THE
WORLD'S DUMBEST
CRIMINALS

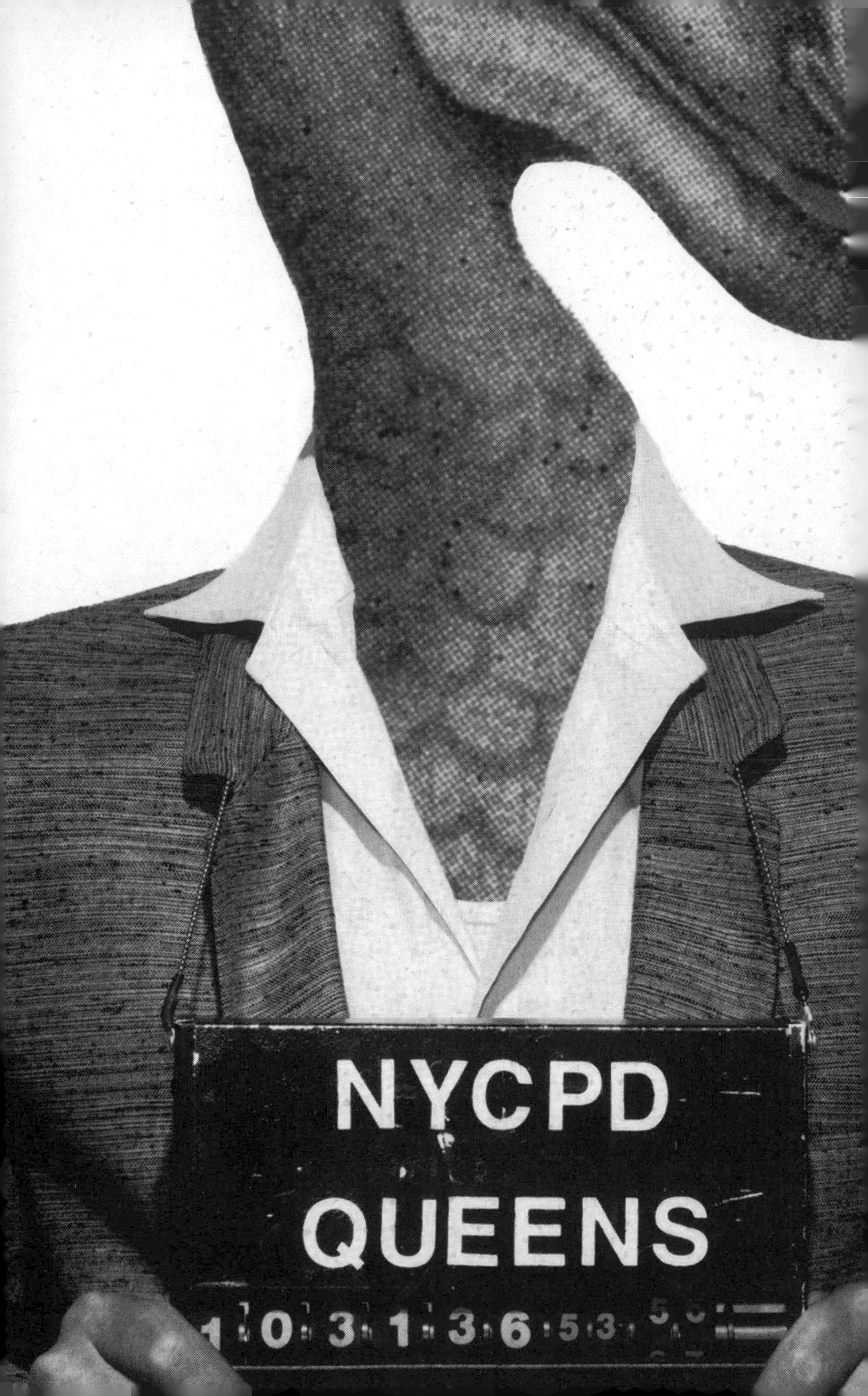
NYCPD
QUEENS

THE
WORLD'S DUMBEST
CRIMINALS

Outrageously True Stories of Criminals
Committing Stupid Crimes

HARPERCOLLINS PUBLISHERS LTD

Published by HarperCollins Publishers Ltd

First edition

HarperCollins Publishers Ltd
Bay Adelaide Centre, East Tower
22 Adelaide Street West, 41st Floor
Toronto, Ontario, Canada
M5H 4E3

www.harpercollins.ca

Library and Archives Canada Cataloguing in Publication
Title: The world's dumbest criminals : outrageously true stories of
criminals committing stupid crimes.
Identifiers: Canadiana (print) 20200193414 | Canadiana (ebook) 20200193449 |
ISBN 9781443459396   (softcover) | ISBN 9781443459402 (ebook)
Subjects: LCSH: Criminals—Humor. | LCSH: Crime—Humor. | LCSH: Criminals—Case studies.
Classification: LCC HV6030 .W67 2020 | DDC 364.1—dc23

Printed and bound in the United States of America
LSC 9 8 7 6 5 4 3 2 1

"In a world of thieves, the only final sin is stupidity."

—HUNTER S. THOMPSON, *FEAR AND LOATHING IN LAS VEGAS*

CONTENTS

AUTHOR'S NOTE

Pseudonyms have been used to protect the identities of various individuals mentioned in this book where warranted or deemed appropriate in the circumstances. Any name that appears in quotation marks the first time it appears in the book is a pseudonym and not the real name of the person so identified.

PREFACE

What is it about dumb criminals that is so endlessly entertaining? Perhaps it starts with the criminality. Criminals are bad, and everyone is fascinated by bad men and women. Witness the appeal of such badly flawed characters as Cleopatra, Grendel, Jack the Ripper, Jesse James, Catherine the Great, Rasputin and Charles Manson. (Some might be tempted to add Donald Trump to this list, but history will have the final word on him.)

Then there's the dumbness. It is always amusing to see or hear about other people's blunders, whether through faulty planning or clumsy execution. That's why Wile E. Coyote never catches the Road Runner. That's why Kevin McCallister always foils those burglars.

So dumb criminals make for perfect light reading. When a hero fails, it's tragedy, but when a criminal fails, it's comedy, a relief, plus someone getting their just deserts. You don't need to feel sad or guilty or anything except amused when a bad guy flops, and you can throw in a bit of moral superiority if you need to.

So here you go. Amuse yourself with a selection of flops, fails and fiascos from around the world. Most of the time, the criminals involved deserve to be laughed at, and they always deserve to fail.

THE
WORLD'S DUMBEST
CRIMINALS

THEY DIDN'T BANK ON GETTING CAUGHT

NICKELED AND DIMED

There was obviously very little brain power put into planning this robbery. Either that or the getaway driver put so much brain power into it that it tired him out. One way or another, police found him asleep outside the bank in question.

Let's start at the beginning. On a Sunday morning in June 2017, three men decided to rob a bank. The plan, as far as anyone can tell, was to go as follows: two of the men would break into a Wachovia bank in South Beach, Florida, and the third member of the gang would wait behind the wheel of the getaway car.

According to *NBC 6*, the two got into the bank by smashing the window at 5:45 a.m. on a Sunday. The bank, of course, was closed, and all the cash was locked in the vault. It appears the men did not have the foresight to realize that this would be the case. So after finding out that all the cash was locked away, they decided to improvise, taking all the quarters, dimes and nickels they could carry. Turns out, they couldn't handle as many as they thought they could. They filled some bags and headed for the car, but the coins weighed them down so much they were easily caught by the police.

Meanwhile, their getaway driver had fallen asleep, drunk, behind the wheel, and even slept through the sirens and the arrival of the cops.

CALLING AHEAD FOR TAKEOUT

Two would-be bank robbers tried "phoning in" a heist, presumably to increase efficiency and their chances of success, according to Connecticut police. Not surprisingly, their plan backfired.

"I've heard of drive-up robberies where they rob the bank via drive-up windows," said Detective Lieutenant Michael Gagner of the Fairfield Police Department. "But I've never had somebody call ahead and say, 'Get the money, we're coming.'"

The attempted bank job occurred in March 2010 at a branch of the People's Bank in Fairfield. According to a CNN report, a bank employee received a phone call from one of the suspects demanding that $100,000 in large bills be gathered. The suspect threatened that there would be a "blood bath" if their demands were not met.

The employee immediately called 911, Gagner reported. The bank also initiated a lockdown; however, one of the robbers was already inside. While his co-conspirator was on the phone with one teller, he had entered the bank and handed another teller a note demanding money. "The [employee] is literally giving us a blow-by-blow, saying the robbery is going down," Gagner said.

The suspect in the bank was able to take around $900, but by the time he asked employees to open the door for him to leave, police had arrived at the scene. The suspect ignored the officers' orders to stop and ran to a nearby car, where his partner was waiting. Police were then able to arrest both suspects without incident.

As reported by the *Fairfield Citizen*, a search by police of the suspects' vehicle produced a scanner tuned to the Fairfield police frequency, two walkie-talkies and a robbery to-do list that included times for getting into and out of the bank.

"We were all kind of cracking up with the call-ahead aspect of it," Gagner said. "Definitely unusual technique."

Gagner added that the robbers had insisted that a dye pack not be put in with the money waiting for them. The bank disregarded this order, and a bag of cash got covered in dye when it was thrown on the ground.

One of the suspects was a twenty-seven-year-old man, "Arnold," from Bridgeport, Connecticut. The other was his sixteen-year-old cousin, who was considered a juvenile. The two were charged with first-degree robbery and threatening in the first degree.

In October 2010, Arnold pleaded guilty in Connecticut State Superior Court to conspiracy to commit second-degree robbery, being a persistent dangerous felony offender and harassment.

Arnold was on probation at the time, having served seven years for another bank holdup in July 2003. According to prosecutor Howard Stein, Arnold had walked into a bank and handed the teller a note demanding $50,000 in cash, saying that he had a bomb. Upon leaving the bank, Arnold was immediately arrested. Police found a circuit board and some wires in his pocket, Stein said. Arnold told police he had been kidnapped by a man who said he was putting a bomb in Arnold's pocket and threatened to detonate it unless he robbed the bank for him. Despite this story, Arnold ended up pleading guilty to that robbery too.

A FAMILY AFFAIR

"Roland" was a widower who had a problem with alcohol and a pile of bills. He also had two kids. So he did what most struggling dads do when they are trying to support their families: he got a handgun and held up a bank.

According to police reports, after that first successful bank robbery, every year or so, Roland would visit a bank and steal a few thousand dollars. It paid the bills.

After robbing five banks, Roland moved from Oregon to Texas, and his twenty-year-old son, "Dean," and eighteen-year-old daughter, "Bibi," soon followed. Roland wanted to start a gang, so he asked his kids to help out. Dean needed money for college, so he was willing. Bibi also agreed, but mostly just to please her dad.

According to *HuffPost*, the family robbed their first bank, in Katy, Texas, in August 2012. Roland and Dean wore painter's masks and overalls, and carried pellet guns. Bibi parked behind the building and waited for them, keeping in touch by phone.

The robbery netted nearly $70,000. A few months later, they pulled a second job, but this time they made a mistake when they tried to case the bank in advance. Wearing orange safety vests, they pretended to be construction workers who wanted to open accounts. After the robbery, detectives viewing the security videos thought the vests were too clean to belong to real construction workers. *Oxygen* reported that the police tracked the vests to a local hardware store and got Roland's credit card information. They busted the family in November.

As reported by *ABC News*, the robbers immediately confessed. Because Bibi was merely the getaway driver, and under duress, she was sentenced to five years. Dean was given a ten-year sentence, and Roland, who also confessed to several robberies in Oregon, got twenty-four years.

Dean and Bibi said they hoped to start new lives once they got out of jail, though their father would be in prison for a long time.

Bibi was arrested again in August 2016 for participating in an armed robbery at a gas station in Laredo, Texas, *Oxygen* reported. She had been released for good behavior in October 2015 after serving two years and ten months of her sentence. Laredo police said she was sitting inside a vehicle in the parking lot outside the store when they were called to answer an armed-robbery report. Bibi was arrested when officers learned she was on parole for the 2012 robberies.

BUTTED OUT

A bank robber from Ambridge, Pennsylvania, will spend ten years in prison because he really, really needed a smoke.

According to *The Times*, on October 4, 2013, the police were in pursuit of thirty-eight-year-old "Peter" after the robbery of the Huntington Bank in Ambridge. Officers stopped and gave a group of construction workers a description of the man they were after. Just moments later, Peter stopped and asked one of the construction workers for a cigarette. The worker provided the cigarette and, not knowing who Peter was, mentioned that the police were searching for someone wearing a cap and a blue shirt. Peter then nervously removed his blue shirt and baseball cap and threw them in a large waste container nearby.

Peter's smoke break gave police time to find him, and they arrested him shortly thereafter.

In June 2014, Peter pleaded guilty in a Pittsburgh courtroom, facing a sentence of as much as twelve years in prison, according to federal guidelines. Senior U.S. District Judge Gustave Diamond gave him ten years.

At the time of the Huntington Bank robbery, Peter was on

probation for robbing another Ambridge bank in March 2008. In that case, the teller had put a dye pack in with the money. Several hours later, police pulled a car over because the driver was wanted on a parole violation, and found Peter in the vehicle, covered in dye.

The thief apparently learned one lesson from that earlier crime: when he entered the Huntington Bank, he told the teller, "This is a robbery. No dye packs. No alarms."

RED-LETTER DAY

A Pensacola, Florida, man pleaded guilty in April 2011 to stealing almost $10,000 from a bank. His fatal error was that he returned to the bank to retrieve the note he had handed to a teller.

The would-be thief walked into a Regions Bank in Foley, Alabama, in October 2010 and slipped a note to the teller. "I have a gun," the note read. "Do not alert anyone. No alarms, no dye packs, give me all the money in your drawer. You have 15 seconds, do not panic or alert anyone."

According to his plea agreement, the thirty-three-year-old robber left the bank with $9,945 but returned to retrieve the holdup note, reported *AL.com*.

A Baldwin County sheriff's deputy was able to catch up to the man, who was driving a stolen black Ford Explorer, and chase him until the vehicle overturned. All of the money was recovered, as was the stickup note.

INTERVIEW WITH A BANK ROBBER

A resident of Lawrenceville, Georgia, thought he was being a helpful and engaged citizen when he agreed to do an on-camera interview with a local news station to talk about public transit. However, he might have been able to sell the helpful and engaged citizen role with more conviction had he not just robbed a Chase Bank minutes before. Witnesses saw him leave the bank and walk toward the news truck. Upon agreeing to do the interview, he removed his bank robbery disguise (his hat and do-rag) and revealed his face to the camera—and the world.

The manager of the bank told the police where he believed the suspect had gone. When the officers followed up with the TV station, they learned that the interviewee had given the reporter his real name.

After the interview, the thief proceeded to case a Fidelity Bank in the area, authorities later revealed. It is believed that he tried to rob five banks in all but got money from only two of them.

In a Facebook post, the Lawrenceville Police Department offered some advice to those considering a career in bank robbery. "When after having robbed several banks and you are at another bank casing the place for an additional robbery and are approached by a news crew in the parking lot . . . DO NOT stop and agree to an interview with said news crew," the statement read. "You see, when you accept an interview and provide them with your real name it actually makes our job too easy."

TATTLE TELLER

A bank robber walked into a Bank of America branch in San Francisco and wrote a note that read, "This iz a stikkup. Put all your muny in this bag." But then, worried that someone had seen him write the note and would call the cops, he walked out, crossed the road to a Wells Fargo bank and went up to a teller with the note.

As reported by *The Telegraph*, the Wells Fargo teller told the robber she couldn't accept his stickup note because it was written on a Bank of America deposit slip. He would either have to fill out a Wells Fargo deposit slip or go back to Bank of America.

Defeated, he said "Okay" and left. The teller called the cops, who found him in the lineup back at the Bank of America.

This robber's note-writing style contrasts dramatically with that of the "Good Grammar Bandit," who robbed a series of banks in Colorado. According to *CBS Denver*, in 2015 police finally managed to arrest a man who had penned immaculately written robbery notes that were typed and used proper spelling, grammar and punctuation. He obviously did not want to risk any miscommunication.

WILD KINGDOM

THAT'LL TEACH HIM

After a two-day search of Kruger National Park in South Africa for the body of a suspected poacher, officials recovered only two items: a skull and a pair of pants.

In April 2019, the suspected poacher had entered the park with a group of other men to illegally hunt rhinoceros when, according to his accomplices, he was trampled by an elephant. As if this message from Mother Nature wasn't clear enough, park officials believe the man's body was then "devoured" by a pride of lions, *TimesLIVE* reported.

"Entering Kruger National Park illegally and on foot is not wise, it holds many dangers and this incident is evidence of that," said Glenn Phillips, managing executive of the park.

Reports vary on the number of accomplices the suspected poacher entered the park with; depending on which source is correct, either three or four men have been arrested and are awaiting trial.

According to *TimesLIVE*, Kruger National Park has an ongoing problem with poaching, and there remains a strong demand for rhino horn, which some people believe is an aphrodisiac. The park is home to both black and white species of rhinoceros. The World Wildlife Fund lists both species as vulnerable, and Save the Rhino lists black rhinos as critically endangered, with fewer than 6,000 left in the wild.

The same week the poacher died, Hong Kong airport authorities seized the biggest haul of rhino horns in five years, valued at $2.1 million.

CAN I TAKE A MESSAGE?

Homing pigeons have been used to carry messages for thousands of years, as their powerful "homing" ability enables them to return to their lofts even if they are hundreds of miles away. Pigeons are mentioned in the Bible and were used to deliver chariot-racing results across the Roman Empire. As Genghis Khan went about conquering the world, he set up pigeon relay stations along the way. *The New York Times* noted that France, quite aware of the carrier pigeon's ability, mobilized 30,000 pigeons during the First World War and made a law that those who interfered with the pigeons' flight would be sentenced to death.

So, given the great ability and history of pigeons, it was just a matter of time before someone attempted to use them for smuggling in the modern era.

One smuggler pigeon was caught in Kuwait in 2017. The captured pigeon was found to be carrying 178 ketamine pills, an anesthetic also used recreationally, in a tiny backpack. Kuwaiti customs officials were already aware of pigeons' roles in the drug-smuggling industry, but as reported by the BBC, "this was the first time they had caught a bird in the act."

Officials in other countries have seen similar cases in which pigeons are used as accomplices to those trying to smuggle lightweight, high-value narcotics. Some groups have created organized pigeon operations: in 2017 *The Guardian* reported that authorities in Iran had confiscated 100 carrier pigeons from an individual who had trained them to fly to a specific location with small bags of illegal substances attached to their legs.

Others have less formulated approaches: in 2011 Colombian police discovered a pigeon that couldn't manage to fly over a prison wall because of the weight of the cocaine and marijuana strapped to it. "We found the bird about a block away from the prison trying to fly over with a package, but due to the excess weight it could not accomplish its mission," a police spokesman said.

The Colombian police were unsurprised by this attempt, citing past use of carrier pigeons to smuggle phone SIM cards into jails, reported *The Guardian*.

The bird captured by Kuwaiti officials was cared for by the local ecological police unit, officers said.

PENGUIN PLAY

Dirk, a fairy penguin from a theme park in Queensland, Australia, was rescued and returned home, safe and sound, after he was abducted by two inebriated men.

Three men were charged with trespassing and stealing the penguin after their Facebook posts about their rowdy night were shown to police. A twenty-one-year-old and a twenty-year-old admitted breaking into Sea World, on Queensland's Gold Coast, swimming with the dolphins and letting off a fire extinguisher in the shark enclosure. To top off their night, they decided to steal Dirk.

The penguin-nappers, both from Wales, pleaded guilty to trespassing, and stealing and keeping a protected animal, Australia's Department of Justice said. The eighteen-year-old Australian man who was with them was charged with trespassing and was to be sentenced at a later date.

The magistrate accepted an appeal not to record convictions against the two Welshmen and fined them each $1,000.

The men's lawyer told Southport Magistrates Court that they tried "their incompetent best" to care for Dirk by feeding him and putting him in the shower. They later released him into a canal, from which he was rescued.

Dirk was raised in captivity and had never lived in the wild. "Had we not got him it wouldn't have been a good situation at all in the long term for Dirk," said Sea World's director of marine sciences, Trevor Long.

After his rescue, Dirk, who is part of a breeding colony, was reunited with his girlfriend, Peaches. The seven-year-old penguin was "in reasonable health, although exhausted" when he made it home, officials from Sea World said.

Magistrate Brian Kucks was told that, while the tourists' actions were undoubtably immature and stupid, there was no malice involved.

Kucks told the men, "You could have found yourselves in a morgue if you'd gone into the wrong enclosure. Perhaps next time you are at a party you will consider drinking a little less vodka."

MAN'S BEST (IMAGINARY) FRIEND

On three different occasions, Police Constable Steven Hutton has captured suspects by using an imaginary dog to slow them down.

In the most recent incident, in April 2017, PC Hutton was searching for a man near Salisbury, England, who had breached a court order. Hutton was parked on a building site when he spotted the man. As reported by the *Swindon Advertiser*, Hutton loudly proclaimed that he had a police dog and told the man to turn himself in. Hutton made a show of shouting "Sit," "Stay" and "Lie down" into the open back of his car. Unbeknownst to the suspect, the constable was alone.

Hutton said, "I knew the guy would stay still if I could convince him I had a dog. He couldn't see into the back of my car, so I just walked around to the back and told my imaginary dog to keep still. Luckily, I didn't have to bark this time. When the suspect walked past my car, after we had arrested him, he then realized what had happened and that I didn't have a dog."

Hutton had previously arrested a man in June 2016 by barking like a dog after a high-speed chase ended on foot, reported *USA Today*. In that incident, Hutton and other Wiltshire police officers had tried to pull over a speeding vehicle in Swindon. Police then used a tire-deflation "stinger" to stop the car, and the four young occupants fled on foot. As Hutton chased one of the men, he decided to shout that he had a dog, adding a "few fake barks," which incited the man to surrender.

"He stopped and we got up to him before he realized there wasn't a dog and he was arrested," Hutton said. "By the look on his face you could see he was a little bit disappointed with himself."

He added, "I've done it before when I was based in Salisbury and we were trying to get a man at a school. He ran across the school field and I knew we were never going to catch him, so I let out a couple of barks."

KITTY KARMA

An Ohio woman got a taste of her own medicine when she was sentenced to spend a night in the woods with only the bare essentials as part of her punishment for abandoning thirty-five kittens in a park.

Painesville Municipal Court Judge Michael A. Cicconetti sentenced "Mindy," twenty-five, in November 2005. Earlier that year, park rangers had found kittens abandoned in two different parks in Mentor, Ohio. Some of the kittens had upper respiratory infections, and nine of them subsequently died. Police had no trouble tracing the kittens back to Mindy, as she had neglected to remove their identification collars.

Members of the community were surprised to hear of Mindy's crime, because she was formerly known as an animal rescuer.

Mindy claimed that someone had left the kittens on her doorstep, and that the local Humane Society had refused to help; however, the Humane Society was quick to refute the allegation.

According to *ABC News*, the judge expressed his disapproval of Mindy's actions during the hearing, saying, "How would you like to be dumped off at a metro park late at night, spend the night listening to the coyotes . . . listening to the raccoons around you in the dark night, and sit out there in the cold not knowing where you're going to get your next meal, not knowing when you are going to be rescued?"

Cicconetti decided to give Mindy a choice: she could receive the standard punishment for domestic animal abandonment—ninety days in jail—or she could choose fourteen days in jail, fifteen days on house arrest, substantial donations to the Humane Society and the park rangers, and one night alone in the woods, just like the kittens she had abandoned.

Mindy agreed to the judge's creative sentencing, and the punishment was to take place on the night before Thanksgiving. She was allowed only the clothes on her back, water and an emergency communication device—no light, no food, no entertainment.

As she was about to set off on her snowy exile in Concord Woods park, Mindy was still notably lacking remorse, reported *ABC News*. "I don't have warm enough clothes and I'm not even allowed to bring a sleeping bag," she complained. "I don't understand how a judge can send me out there to freeze."

As it happened, Cicconetti changed his mind later that night. "I couldn't allow it to go on any further," he said. "I did not want to put her health and safety in jeopardy."

Cicconetti said weather forecasts had convinced him to call Metroparks rangers to bring Mindy inside. Rangers took her to Lake County Jail.

This is not the first time that Judge Cicconetti has matched the sentence to the crime. In fact, over the years he has garnered quite a reputation for giving out creative punishments. As reported by *The Plain Dealer*, in 2002 Cicconetti ruled on a case in which a man called an officer a pig during a confrontation. The judge sentenced the man to stand on the street next to a pig with a sign that read "This is not a police officer." In 2007 he made three men dress up in chicken suits and hold a sign reading "World-Famous Chicken Ranch," referring to a brothel where they had solicited sex.

When it comes to facing justice in Painesville, Ohio, criminals are quite aware that they shouldn't do the crime if they can't do the time— or as the case may be, meet the often-humiliating terms of Judge Cicconetti's sentencing.

ARMORED AND DANGEROUS

In April 2015, when "Lucas" of Lee County, Georgia, saw an armadillo on his property, he decided to shoot it with his 9-mm pistol. As one does.

In the southern United States, armadillos are widely regarded as nuisances; think moles or groundhogs, only bigger and armored. This context is helpful, although the story is still strange.

According to a report from *WALB News*, Lucas, fifty-four, hit the armadillo and killed it, but that's not all he hit. The bullet ricocheted off the animal, hit a fence and went through the back door of a mobile home that was 100 yards away from Lucas. And the bullet still wasn't finished! It then proceeded to go through the back of the reclining chair Lucas's mother-in-law was sitting in, hitting her in the back.

"Just the circumstances, just all the way around, the whole situation was unusual," said Investigator Bill Smith of the Lee County Sheriff's Office.

Luckily, Lucas's seventy-four-year-old mother-in-law wasn't severely injured.

"She was walking around on her own power and talking," Smith said. "It didn't appear to be too severe," he added, although she was taken to the hospital to be on the safe side.

Despite this fiasco, the Dougherty County Extension Coordinator told *WALB News* that shooting armadillos is recommended. "At first I ask if they live in the city or [country]," he said, "because shooting is an effective way of getting rid of them. However, you have to be safe when you do that."

Perhaps unsurprisingly, this is not the only time someone has been injured when shooting an armadillo. That same year, the CBC reported that a man in Texas was injured when his bullet ricocheted off the shell of an armadillo and into his face. While Lucas was at least successful in killing the animal, the Texas man's prey was never located, leaving him with nothing but a broken jaw and a bout of humiliation.

OUTFOXED

It was a mystery. Residents of a neighborhood in the city of Nagaokakyo, Japan, about 235 miles west of Tokyo in the Kyoto prefecture, were placing their footwear in the covered entryways outside their doors—as usual—and the shoes and sandals were going missing. Not surprisingly, the residents were complaining. Dozens of shoes and sandals had been stolen in a two-week period. Who would do such a thing?

Finally, near the end of May 2018, police mounted a surveillance operation with five officers on an overnight stakeout. After six hours, they spotted two foxes roaming around in the backyard of an empty house. An inspection of the foxes' burrow uncovered forty pairs of shoes.

"The two foxes that the police officers spotted could have been building a burrow to breed and collected the sandals out of their instinct to stock up on food and other items," Kyoto City Zoo chief Naoki Yamashita said.

"I can't believe that foxes stole my sandals," said one resident of the neighborhood.

The police sent leaflets to the residents, warning them to keep their footwear indoors to prevent any further thefts.

The Nagaokakyo animals are not the first shoe-stealing foxes. In 2009, authorities in the small town of Föhren, in western Germany, said a fox was responsible for stealing more than a hundred shoes, and in 2014, a resident of Portsmouth, England, reported finding more than fifty shoes, mostly trainers and work boots, along a path near a fox den.

DISGUISE THE LIMIT

EVERYONE LOVES A CLOWN

Two men thought that they had successfully robbed a jewelry store in Denver, Colorado. According to *HuffPost*, the men, dressed as clowns, entered wielding guns and forced the occupants of the store to lie down on the ground. The men then "ransacked" the store, steal ing all the display jewelry in sight. Unfortunately for them, the store keeps fake platinum and gold jewelry in their display cases, meaning the two fools actually made off with a large collection of totally worth-less jewelry. At least they were dressed for the part.

NOT THEIR BAG

Planning a robbery can be a lot of work. And hey, sometimes the lit-tle details are hard to iron out. Still, this robbery attempt is down-right embarrassing.

In Baltimore, Maryland, a man went into a drugstore, waved a gun, announced a robbery and pulled a Hefty bag over his head to mask his face. He then realized that he'd forgotten to cut eyeholes in the bag. He was taken into custody by store security staff.

However, before we get too critical, it seems only fair to mention that poorly planned masks seem to be a common burglary error. As reported by CNN in 2009, two men were seen attempting to rob an apartment in Carroll, Iowa. The men quickly fled the scene. However, when police tracked them down just blocks away, the officers were amused to find that the men's only disguise was permanent black marker scribbled across their faces in a ridiculously ineffective attempt to draw masks.

The presiding judge dismissed the charges against the two in November 2009, saying there was insufficient evidence to convict them. There was no evidence they had entered the apartment, he said; moreover, neither man had a weapon and no one was injured.

Mug shots released by the police show the black ink scribbles on the suspects' faces, in what some commentators described as "the worst disguise ever."

In an interview with CNN, Carroll Police Chief Jeff Cayler said: "We're very skilled investigators and the [drawn-on] faces gave them right away. I have to assume the officers were kind of laughing at the time. I've never heard of coloring your face with a permanent marker."

QUEUE THE ROBBER

"Steven," thirty-eight, stood patiently in line at a bank in Bishop Auckland, England, for fifteen minutes. Although it was a hot day, he wore blue latex gloves, a jacket with the hood pulled up, a face mask and dark glasses. He was also carrying a large bottle of Febreze and a holdall. All in all, it was definitely not the subtlest approach to a disguise.

Unsurprisingly, as Durham Crown Court was told in December 2018, Steven presented such an odd figure that another bank customer felt concerned and suspicious, and decided to take a photo of him.

The bank's manager was also worried by the strange customer, but she didn't want to offend him if he needed his outfit because of a skin condition. Besides, he was waiting his turn so patiently; surely a bank robber wouldn't do that!

When Steven eventually reached the counter, he handed a note to the cashier telling her he had acid and a bomb. According to *The Telegraph*, the terrified teller bundled £370 into Steven's holdall. Steven then left the bank.

The cashier had her wits about her enough to give Steven a fake money packet containing a tracking device. Unfortunately, the device was broken. But members of the public took note of the getaway car, giving the police details of its appearance that led to Steven's capture.

Court records reveal that Steven had researched bank robbery techniques on Google and used his girlfriend's car for the heist while she was walking her dog. He drove to the NatWest bank branch and, instead of going straight to the desk, chose to stand in line.

"Suspicions were aroused because of the appearance of the defendant and the fact he was rather obviously trying to avoid the security cameras," prosecutor Jane Waugh said. "One customer said he 'didn't look quite right,' and the police were called because of their suspicions. The manager approached the defendant as he waited in the queue and asked if she could help him. He replied 'no.'"

Steven, of West Auckland, admitted robbery and taking his girlfriend's car without consent. He was jailed for three years and four months by Judge Christopher Prince, who described the robbery as planned but unsophisticated.

The judge did not want to criticize anyone in the bank for their actions that day, but he did regret "that more was not done to spare [the teller] from the situation that arose. She was left to face [Steven] one to one over the counter and was left in fear as to what might happen."

The court heard that the teller spent months off work after the incident and was only just then returning to duty. In a report by *Metro*, she revealed that she relived the heist in nightmares, which kept her awake.

"There were children in the bank in pushchairs, other staff and numerous customers. We all could have been hurt by the actions of this person."

The manager also made a statement after the robbery, saying, "My staff were terrified. I feel nervous for the staff and nervous opening up the branch."

Steven's lawyer told the court that Steven had suffered a brain injury three years before that had caused him "cognitive difficulties," adding that he also had addictions to gambling and alcohol. As a further mitigating factor, the lawyer noted, the Febreze bottle had actually contained Febreze, not acid.

Steven wrote letters to the bank's staff, saying he was "genuinely sorry" for the robbery.

BURGLAR BAGGED

A burglar in India was arrested after using a transparent plastic bag to mask his face.

In March 2018, *NewsX* obtained video surveillance footage showing the man breaking into the Anisika mobile phone shop in Kanyakumari, in Tamil Nadu. The thief's face and beard could easily be seen through the plastic bag as he climbed over the counter to get at the merchandise, an act that, of course, left his fingerprints everywhere. He also gave the camera a clear view of the heart-shaped tattoo just above his thumb.

According to *NewsX*, the shop's owner went to work the next day to find about $2,500 worth of phones and accessories missing. Luckily for the owner, the thief was not difficult to find.

Police arrested a youth from the area in connection with the burglary.

SOCK IT TO THEM

A twenty-seven-year-old man from Treorchy, Wales, went to a Barclays Bank branch in 2014 to inform them of his new address, as any responsible adult does. But when he saw money behind the counter, it was too tempting for him.

He returned half an hour later, planning to rob the bank, dressed in a "terrible disguise": sunglasses and socks over his shoes. Having already been to the bank that day, it was a sloppy move on his part not to bother changing his clothes. Also, no one could really explain the thought process behind the socks-over-shoes part. The cashier refused to give him any money, instead pressing her panic button, and the man ran away empty-handed.

South Wales Police quickly tracked him down, however, because he had conveniently told the cashier his full name and new address during his earlier visit.

In Merthyr Crown Court, the man admitted attempted robbery and carrying a bladed weapon, and was jailed for two-and-a-half years.

The defense lawyer said, "He told the police it was stupid and he was very sorry, but he was desperate for money."

He was certainly correct about the "stupid" part.

HE WAS A BAD MAN

A man from Brackla, Wales, was sentenced to sixteen months in jail for the burglary of the Marine Hotel in Porthcawl during an Elvis Festival.

"Charlie," thirty-seven, was reported by South Wales Police as having entered the hotel at around 2:00 a.m. on September 27, 2015, wearing a shopping bag on his head as a disguise. He can be seen in CCTV surveillance cameras walking through the hotel, and was caught by a guest who woke up to find Charlie in his room, trying to steal his laptop computer.

According to local police, Charlie fled, but they were able to identify him on the CCTV footage because he stupidly decided to remove his shopping bag "mask" and look into the camera lens from a few feet away. He was soon arrested.

Charlie admitted the burglary, though he didn't actually steal anything, and was ordered to pay £900 court costs and a £100 surcharge.

MY FELLOW AUSTRIANS

A mused bank staff who were participating in a training session on an early-closing day in 2009 watched as a would-be robber hammered on the door with his gun, demanding to be let in.

Police in Kirchheim, Austria, said the robber, who was wearing a Barack Obama mask, finally fled empty-handed and drove away.

A bank spokesperson said, "He wasn't very smart. The bank was robbed both last December and in January this year and we now have really tight security."

According to the *Daily Mail*, in March 2011, police arrested the man they believe was responsible for the Kirchheim incident. They said he had robbed half a dozen banks in the province of Upper Austria since 2008, always wearing an Obama mask.

The man, nicknamed the "Obama robber" by the media, was captured after he hit a branch near the town of Voecklabruck, holding a bank employee at gunpoint before fleeing in a car, police said.

It is thought he carried out his first robbery in November 2008 in Weilbach, but it wasn't until December 2009 that he donned the Obama mask for his attempt to rob the bank in Kirchheim.

THINGS GO BETTER WITH . . .

There's a definite and clear line between a robber's disguise and a Halloween costume. But a pistol-packing crook from Kentucky might disagree after he successfully robbed a fast-food restaurant dressed as a Coca-Cola bottle.

As reported by *CBS Sacramento*, the man made off with $500 after threatening a Rally's manager who was opening up at 7 a.m. and was the only person in the restaurant. Surveillance video shows the manager opening the back door to give a bag of food to the giant Coke bottle, who then barged into the restaurant. He waved a handgun at the manager but did not shoot it.

After exiting the restaurant, the super-sized soda got into a gray minivan and fled.

DRIVEN BY CRIME

RECKLESS ABANDON

A Brooklyn woman recently found out the hard way that lying to police about a child abduction just so they will find your car faster is, in fact, a crime. According to the *New York Post*, the woman's car was stolen when she left it idling at the side of the road. In a scheme to get police to work faster on her case, the woman told the responding officers that her six-year-old nephew was in the back of the car when it was stolen. Police were predictably unimpressed when, ten minutes later, the vehicle was located parked on the side of the road, sans child. The nephew had been safe at home while the investigation was taking place. The woman was charged with filing a false police report.

HELLO, DOLLY

In January 2018, a California driver tried to get around the carpool lane rules, which require a car to be carrying at least one passenger in order to drive in the faster, far-left lane. His grand plan? He strapped a Chucky doll (you know, like the one from the *Child's Play* movies) into his passenger seat.

But it didn't work. According to *The Kansas City Star*, during a traffic slowdown, a Contra Costa Highway Patrol officer noticed the terrifying doll and wrote the driver a ticket. Violations can carry a fine of as much as $500.

The officer snapped a photo of the "passenger" and posted it on Facebook, saying, "[T]his will definitely not work as your carpool passenger! But hilarious! A for effort . . . and here's your carpool ticket. (This seriously happened . . . c'mon people.)"

The driver's name was not released.

YOU'RE MANNEQUIN A MISTAKE

One traffic laws violator must've felt like a dummy when he was pulled over by police in Brea, California, after swerving out of the carpool lane one evening in September 2016.

As reported by the *Los Angeles Times*, a police officer on a motorcycle pulled up to the driver's open window, planning on giving him a warning to be more careful when changing lanes. And that's when he saw it: the truck's "passenger" was a female mannequin in a hoodie, presumably placed there to let the man fake his way into the carpool lane.

The driver admitted that he had been using the mannequin for this purpose for a while, Brea police said, but this time he was issued a citation for his carpool lane violation. From now on, he would have to drive in the slow lanes like everyone else.

"Nice try," the Brea Police Department tweeted.

MORTGAGING HIS FUTURE

Police hit the jackpot when they pulled over a car for speeding and discovered that the two men inside were in possession of £980,000 in cash.

As the *Manchester Evening News* reported, the eventual result was that "Abdul," thirty-nine, pleaded guilty in Manchester Crown Court to charges of laundering money for dangerous criminals and for scamming £345,000 from a bank for a phony mortgage. He was sentenced in January 2017 to six years in prison. Abdul's associate was sentenced to twenty months for money laundering. Both men were from the Manchester area.

After the traffic stop, police raided Abdul's home in Hyde, Greater Manchester, in September 2014 and found evidence that he had laundered £1.3 million for criminal gangs in just seven months. Another £116,000 in cash was found at the associate's Moston home.

On top of that, detectives later learned that Abdul had lied to a bank about his salary when applying for a mortgage on a property in Altrincham in 2009. Because he wasn't making as much as he claimed, he was unable to pay the mortgage and the house was repossessed.

Detective Constable Richard Hudd of the Greater Manchester Police said, "Not only has [Abdul] used deception to swindle the bank into lending him large amounts of money for a mortgage, he has also helped dangerous criminals launder illicit cash. Money laundering allows money from illegitimate sources, usually from the proceeds of crime, to enter the system and continue to fund criminal enterprise.

"We will continue to deploy all the resources at our disposal to eliminate this practice, which allows criminals to spread misery on our streets. I hope that this sentence shows that [Abdul's] greed, duplicity and disregard for the communities of Greater Manchester will not be tolerated."

PANTLESS IN QUEENS

In March 2019, New York Police Department officers responded to reports of a "pantless, knife-wielding man" threatening people outside of a precinct station house in Queens. According to *The New York Times*, the man had crashed his SUV into a police vehicle and then attempted to set fire to both cars.

No one can confirm why he had a knife or why he started the blaze—or, indeed, why he thought this was all best done pantless.

In an official statement, a spokesman for the NYPD, Chief of Patrol Rodney Harrison, told *Newsweek* that the man, who was naked from the waist down and wore a fisherman's vest, got out of his car and poured "accelerant fluid" on both cars, then set his vehicle on fire. The NYPD car did not catch fire, so the only real damage done was to his own belongings.

As officers came out of the station house and approached the suspect, he charged them holding a twelve-inch kitchen knife. Two officers responded to the imminent threat by shooting the man in the chest and leg, Harrison reported. The nude firebug was later said to be in stable condition at New York-Presbyterian Queens Hospital.

"When somebody crashes their car and lights up a vehicle, there's the possibility that there may be some mental issues," Harrison theorized to the press.

Upon searching the scene, officers found a blood-covered knife with a hole in the blade—it had seemingly been hit by one of the bullets fired by police. Harrison said, "Regarding who the blood is from, we don't know. No one was stabbed."

Two of the officers who responded to the incident were treated for tinnitus (ringing in the ears).

DEAD ON ARRIVAL

The "Boucher" family was driving home to Quebec from a vacation in Florida when, tragically, the eighty-seven-year-old patriarch died, apparently of a heart attack.

They had just begun their 1,500-mile journey home, but the wife and son did not want to face the cost and aggravation of engaging with the U.S. medical system, or the paperwork involved in bringing a body across the Canada–United States border. So they decided to just keep driving to their Ormstown home, a few miles north of the border in Quebec's Montérégie region, reported Post Media News in association with *The Guardian*.

But they didn't manage to make it across the border. At about 2:30 a.m. on April 1, 2019, when they reached the border at Hemmingford, Quebec, the Bouchers were stopped and searched, and the body was discovered propped up in the back seat of the car. Authorities said he had apparently been dead for at least a day before the Bouchers reached the border crossing.

According to Postmedia News, one border official said it was a "first."

The senior Boucher had reportedly begun to experience serious health problems near the beginning of the twenty-four-hour trip.

Police said they would be performing an autopsy, but the body showed no signs of violence and the man appeared to have suffered a cardiac arrest.

The Bouchers' reluctance to submit to the U.S. health-care system is perfectly understandable, and to be fair, this doesn't really qualify as a stupid crime—it's more just weird, or even simply practical. U.S. hospital stays have been known to send uninsured Canadians into bankruptcy. In one recent case, a man who had a serious automobile accident was presented with a bill for $325,000; in another, a woman who gave birth prematurely in the United States ended up owing almost $1 million.

COPPING A PLEA

"Joey" was not having a good day. In August 2014, the twenty-nine-year-old Florida resident was pulled over by a Collier County deputy for running a stop sign. According to the police report, Joey denied the charge and started arguing with the deputy, who had witnessed the traffic violation and was having none of it.

Joey, of Immokalee, Florida, became so annoyed by how long it was taking the deputy to write him a ticket that he pulled out his phone and dialed 911 to complain, NBC2 reported.

The dispatcher contacted the deputy to confirm the situation, and Joey was arrested and charged with misuse of the emergency phone system. He was released from jail after posting a $2,000 bond.

The deputy admitted that the ticket-issuing process took longer than usual, but blamed the delay on the device that creates the ticket.

OOPS!

HE HAD BANKED ON IT

Most robbers would probably agree that it's a good idea to do at least a little pre-robbery canvasing before committing to looting a place. Apparently, a fifty-seven-year-old German man was too quick to overlook this step when he attempted to hold up a bank that had closed seventeen years earlier, prompting the tabloid newspaper *Bild* to call him "Germany's dumbest bank robber."

The man arrived at the building wielding a toy gun in May 2011. In the lobby, he seized a woman and used her as a hostage to demand €10,000 in ransom from employees, *BBC News* reported.

"This plan failed, however, due to the fact that the building has not held a bank for more than a decade and is now a physiotherapy practice," the court trying him said in a statement.

The building was equipped with ATMs, which could have been part of the reason the suspect was so terribly confused.

"After the defendant recognized the situation, he changed his plan and demanded a passerby withdraw money from the cash machine," the court said. "She withdrew €400 and the defendant made off with the cash in a car he had stolen."

According to *Bild*, the suspect abandoned the vehicle but forgot his toy gun, which was covered with his fingerprints.

The man confessed to the robbery after being interrogated by police, and he received a seven-year sentence due to previous convictions.

IT'S A KNOCKOUT!

When choosing an accomplice for a criminal scheme, you might want to be certain they're actually competent.

A man in Shanghai didn't figure this out until he was hit over the head with it. He and another man were caught on surveillance video approaching a business with bricks in their hands, obviously planning to smash the window and enter the building. The first man threw his brick, but failed to break the glass. His accomplice, eager to help, threw the second brick without waiting for his partner to get out of the way. The brick hit the first man in the head, knocking him unconscious.

Local police were amused by the attempt, *Global News* reported. "If all thieves operated on this level, the police wouldn't have to work overtime," the police statement read.

A BLOODY MESS

Some people are natural burglars, being sly and quick with their hands and often their wits. Others, like "Derek" of Abington, England, are not.

If Derek, forty-six, had any kind of plan when he set out to commit a burglary in February 2013, it was poorly thought out. Things went wrong from the beginning, as the first house he tried to break into had a lock he couldn't pick. In fact, while attempting to break it, he cut his hand and bled all over the place.

So, according to the *Northampton Chronicle & Echo*, he tried again. This time, Derek targeted a nearby house that, conveniently, already had a broken window. He thought the robbery would be a piece of cake and reached through the window to let himself in. If he had been paying a bit more attention, Derek might have realized that the window was broken because the house had been robbed earlier that night, and there were police on the premises interviewing the victim of the earlier crime.

By the time Derek realized his mistake, it was too late. While trying to flee, he was easily caught and arrested. Furthermore, the blood on the scene of his first robbery attempt helped police tie him to that crime as well.

Described by his counsel as "clumsy," Derek was nevertheless sentenced to two-and-a-half years in jail.

TIME FOR A NEW CAREER

"Jason's" foray into armed robbery didn't begin or end well, and pretty much everything that happened in between was messed up too.

To begin with, Jason, twenty-eight, attempted to rob a Martin's newsagent in Abingdon, England, using a plastic toy gun. During the robbery, he removed his balaclava while standing in front of the shop's CCTV camera. Then, as he was trying to leave the shop, he could not open the door. (He was pushing it, and it opened inward.) When his attempt to leave failed, he tried to kick out the door's glass, but fell backward into a floor display of soft drinks, sending bottles rolling all over the floor. The store manager finally went to Jason's aid and helped him open the door.

Despite this list of boneheaded moves, Jason managed to snatch £138.98 from the till.

The staff knew him because he was a regular customer. He had also robbed the shop just ten days earlier, though he left his balaclava on that time.

It took three hours for police to locate him, which is surprisingly long considering they found him still hanging around the same street, with his balaclava in a pocket, wrote the *Daily Mail*. After he was busted, he started crying and told the arresting officers, "I'm sorry, it's not fair on them. Are they all right?"

In July 2012, Jason was jailed by Oxford Crown Court for three years for this offense.

A month later, new details were released after his sentencing for the earlier robbery in the same shop. According to police reports, that incident had taken place just before closing time one evening in late February, as the supervisor was preparing to leave. Jason shouted, "Give me the money!" while holding something in a green case like it was a gun. He made off with £360.

During the trial, Jason's lawyer said his client had been a dental nurse until three years before, when his fiancée left him and he turned to drugs.

Jason pleaded guilty to the possession of a firearm or imitation firearm, for which he was sentenced to two years, with his two sentences run concurrently.

In the *Daily Mail* report, the detective chief inspector is quoted as saying: "Clearly, [Jason's] actions show that he isn't cut out for a career in crime."

HE'S KIND OF TIED UP
AT THE MOMENT

A hapless burglar was jailed for three years after he was found hanging upside down from a window by his shoelaces.

"Joel," thirty-two, got his foot caught while trying to break into a terraced house in Dartford, Kent, England, in August 2008. The *Daily Mail* reported that Joel was suspended upside down for more than an hour, subject to humiliation as a crowd of neighbors and other witnesses gathered around the house to ridicule him.

Attempting to deny his crime, Joel told the owner of the house that he had been trying to stop another thief when he got stuck. Since he was armed with a hammer, this story seems unlikely. The owner certainly thought so, because he declined to set Joel free and called the police.

The police arrived with paramedics and, together, they managed to free Joel from his shoes and return him to the ground. The officers were laughing as they arrested and handcuffed him and took him off to the police station.

Facing Dartford magistrates the following day, Joel admitted burglary with intent to steal.

At his sentencing hearing in October, Maidstone Crown Court heard that Joel had committed fifty other burglaries or attempted break-ins, and that he was a habitual heroin user with a £20-per-day habit. The defending attorney said Joel's problems stemmed from his "addiction to illicit substances and drink." He added, "It was a pathetic burglary. It's clear he was subject to some public humiliation. The burglary offence was opportunistic, it was not pre-planned. It was the fact he needed money for drugs and alcohol."

In sentencing Joel, the judge is quoted in court documents as saying: "This was an entry, albeit an incompetent and pathetic one, which left him dangling from the window for more than an hour." He noted that Joel possessed "a truly appalling criminal record, much of it related to drug abuse."

Joel was ordered to serve at least half of his three-year sentence, less the fifty-nine days already spent in custody. The sentence also incorporated penalties for two assaults on police officers, two shoplifting thefts and possession of class C drugs.

The homeowner, an air-conditioning engineer who had recently moved into the house, said, "The man must be the world's dumbest thief."

GIVE UP YOUR DAY JOB

You know you are bad at robbery when even the judge doesn't think it's worth giving you a full sentence.

Sixty-one-year-old Englishman "Todd" raided six banks and a bookie over the course of two weeks in 2018, Liverpool Crown Court heard, but left empty-handed in every case but one. According to the *New York Post*, the scarf Todd wore over his mouth during the attempted robberies muffled his voice so much that cashiers could not understand his demands for money. Todd also attempted to convince tellers that he had a gun, but his brush wrapped in tape was not very convincing. The staff refused to give him any money, and one woman was so unafraid of him that she told him to "sod off."

In his one effective robbery, he made off with £380 from a bank in Prescot, Merseyside, leaving a teller "crying hysterically." The court heard that he didn't even realize he had successfully stolen the money until he got to a train station and found it in his bag.

After he was arrested, he told officers he would have continued his bank jobs until he paid off gambling debts amounting to £2,000.

As reported in the *Mirror*, after learning that Todd's sentences for past convictions totaled forty-one years, the presiding judge told Todd: "Fortunately, you're not very good at this. I make it quite clear that if you had been more successful you would have been facing today a discretionary life sentence."

NOT TOO ALARMING

"Carl," forty-seven, of Naples, Florida, may be the nicest, most honest burglar ever. Or he is just plain stupid.

According to Detective Tim Lalor of the Lee County Sheriff's Office, when the alarm went off in the middle of the night at the Junkanoo Bar on Fort Myers Beach, the alarm company made the standard phone call. Carl, who was in the middle of robbing the bar, answered the phone, and when the alarm company employee asked for his name, he gave it.

Carl was unable to provide the bar's alarm password, so police were called, though Carl had left by the time they got there. But he didn't get far, considering he had left his name with the alarm company and was clearly visible committing the robbery on the bar's surveillance video. A bottle of Grand Marnier was missing.

According to *NBC2*, deputies later spotted a man matching the description of the man on the video, and confirmed that it was Carl. They promptly arrested him and charged him with unarmed burglary and petty larceny.

"He admitted to answering the phone and told us how nice and professional the lady from ADT was as he gave his correct name," Lalor said.

Lalor added that Carl had committed the burglary on the night of his birthday—and finished off his celebration at the Lee County Jail.

FAST FOOD

DOUGH!

"**S**ean" didn't want to pay 52 cents for a doughnut, so he slipped it into his sweatshirt and ran.

During the incident, Sean, forty-one, was confronted by an employee of the Country Mart in Farmington, Missouri, but he pushed her out of the way and forced his way through the door.

That 52-cent doughnut nearly cost him thirty years in prison, as reported in an Associated Press article published by *NBC News*.

County Prosecutor Wendy Wexler Horn said the push was the problem. It was classified as an assault, albeit a minor one, which elevated the petty shoplifting charge to a forcible robbery, for which the prison sentence would be between five and fifteen years. Furthermore, Sean, of Park Hills, Missouri, had a lengthy criminal record, including prior felonies, which could have doubled the maximum sentence.

Understandably, there was a public outcry when the possible sentence was revealed, accusing the prosecution of overkill.

Prosecutor Horn and Sean's public defender, Chris Klaverkamp, finally agreed that Sean should be placed on probation and serve ninety days in the county jail, with credit for time already served. Sean ended up pleading guilty to second-degree robbery and getting five years of supervised probation.

Klaverkamp said he and Horn did not come to the plea agreement quickly or without a lot of thought, taking into account the defendant's criminal history and the seriousness of the offense, *CBS News* reported.

Circuit Court Judge Sandy Martinez, who followed the recommendation in sentencing Sean, said there had been a lot of talk about it being "just a doughnut," but she understood the state's position that it was not what he took but how he took it.

So was the sweet treat worth all the trouble? Sean doesn't know. He threw the doughnut away while fleeing the store.

"I'VE GOT KETCHUP, AND I'M NOT AFRAID TO USE IT"

Two thieves in Athens, Greece, decided ketchup was their best offense when robbing a supermarket employee who was taking a cash deposit to the bank.

"The thieves jumped out of the bushes and threw two big bags of ketchup on the front window to stop the car," a police official told Reuters. (Who knew ketchup comes in bags?)

The employee fought off his attackers, and the thieves managed to escape with just €400 of the €140,000 he was carrying. Police later apprehended the two men.

This is not the first time that thieves have used pantry supplies in their attacks. According to *The Hindu,* in 2015 police caught a gang in India whose signature move was to use chili powder to disarm their targets. The gang would reportedly throw the chili powder into their victims' faces before robbing them.

While the chili-powder-in-face technique seems marginally more effective, both cases involve bizarre, and questionable, tactics.

GO EASY ON THE CARBS

Police in Livingston County, Michigan, caught restaurant thieves by following their trail of . . . macaroni salad?

The deputies were called to a Build-A-Burger in 2015 after the restaurant had been broken into and robbed of its cash register and surveillance system. As reported by the *Democrat and Chronicle*, upon searching a nearby hiking and biking path, the officers discovered a whole collection of objects dropped by the thieves, including cash register parts, surveillance system parts, rubber gloves and loose change. These men were dropping things left, right and center.

Most notably, the deputies found what they described as "a steady trail of macaroni salad," which led them right to the suspects.

According to the police statement, "It was later discovered that the suspects stole a large bowl of macaroni salad, which they took turns eating along their escape route."

Presumably, it was amazing macaroni salad.

HE'S IN A PICKLE

A man in Glasgow, Scotland, attempted to rob a bookmaking shop armed with a cucumber, a decision that ultimately landed him forty months in jail.

The BBC reported that the twenty-eight-year-old covered the vegetable with a black sock and waved it at a clerk at the Ladbrokes shop in Glasgow's Shettleston neighborhood, demanding cash.

We have to assume the cucumber was curved enough that it could reasonably have been mistaken for a gun. But then again, maybe not. The bookmaker's employee thought the sock might have been concealing a gun, but still refused to give the man any money.

A detective sergeant who happened to be in the betting shop, intercepted the wannabe robber and knocked him down before arresting him. He then removed the sock from the "weapon," revealing the cucumber.

The man was jailed by the High Court in Glasgow after admitting a charge of assault with intent to rob.

According to the BBC, the cucumber-culprit—a plumber who was making £500 a week—told police the whole thing was a joke. "It was a dare," he said. "Am I getting the jail for this?"

He added: "I think it was quite stupid. I am not a robber. It was a laugh that went too far."

NUDE INTRUDER

It's upsetting enough to find a stranger inside your home. It is undoubtably worse to come home to a stranger sitting naked on your couch, eating your pineapple.

According to a report from *The Palm Beach Post*, when a Florida teacher got home from work in October 2017, there was a naked woman in her living room. The trespasser had eaten her leftovers and some canned pineapple, and had stolen one of her son's white T-shirts.

The homeowner went outside, got into her car in the driveway, locked the doors and called the police. She told them the intruder had followed her to her car and was trying to talk to her through the closed window.

When St. Johns County deputies arrived at the home in St. Augustine, Florida, they found the sixty-three-year-old interloper outside the residence.

"The door was open for me to come inside," she told the officers.

Deputies say she entered through the front door of the home "without permission."

The woman was arrested and charged with second-degree burglary and theft. She was taken to jail after the incident, but released the following day.

THEY WENT THATAWAY

MAKING ASSES OF THEMSELVES

If your heist relies on the speed and efficiency of a donkey, you should know that it's probably not going to go well.

A gang of thieves from Colombia learned this lesson the hard way. First, they abducted Xavi, a ten-year-old donkey, twelve hours before the robbery. Those twelve hours gave them plenty of time to steal, say, a car, but they were apparently committed to the donkey plan.

According to the *Daily News*, the robbery itself took place at 2 a.m. in the tiny town of Juan de Acosta, Colombia, in January 2013. The three men broke into a grocery store, stole various goods, then loaded the items onto Xavi and prepared to make their escape. But Xavi decided not to cooperate. In fact, he protested the whole plan—loudly.

At this point, police were not aware that a robbery had taken place, but Xavi was making such a racket that he attracted the attention of patrol officers. In a panic, the robbers fled—on foot, of course—leaving Xavi and their loot behind.

Police were able to return Xavi to his owner.

DUMB AND DUMBEREST

"Percy" and "Chuck" were both nineteen years old when they decided to rob a bank. They failed miserably, and the poorly executed heist would earn them the international nickname "Dumb and Dumber." It is probably fair to say that nobody ever deserved it more.

As reported by *The Sydney Morning Herald*, in March 2005, the Australian teenagers were living in Vail, Colorado, working for a ski shop and snowboarding in their time off. They banked regularly at the WestStar Bank in Vail Village, which is the one they selected for their gunpoint robbery.

Because the teens were such regulars, the bank employees knew them well and easily recognized them despite the balaclavas they wore to cover their faces. But just in case they had any doubts about who the robbers were, the teens had forgotten to take off their name tags from the the ski shop. And apparently, they didn't pause to consider that their distinctive accents might give them away.

The teens held BB guns instead of real guns, but the robbery turned violent when Chuck knocked one of the female bank tellers to the ground.

Despite all the blunders, they made it out of the bank with $132,000, but they weren't done being dumb criminals just yet. They used a chairlift as their getaway vehicle, taking it up the hill and then coming back down on their snowboards. In an attempt to be subtle, they bought a Rolex watch at a nearby store just after the robbery, paying for it with $5 bills, and tipped a taxi driver $20,000. Police later claimed to have identified them within eight minutes.

Percy and Chuck also took snapshots of themselves with the money, which authorities used as key evidence in their trial.

"The next day we got to the airport early and we still had too much cash to smuggle through customs so we decided to chuck it out, but we decided first we'd take some photos of it," Percy said years later, in an interview with the Australian Broadcasting Corporation's *Australian Story*. "We opened up a few bundles and fanned them out and showed off like idiots, and I remember the whole time taking the photos I just had this weird feeling that this was going to come back to haunt me, and sure enough it did."

At the airport, the teens tried to buy one-way tickets to Mexico—with cash, of course. Thanks to a previous incident for which they were wanted for vandalism, they were recognized by airport security and quickly busted.

Percy was sentenced to four-and-a-half years in federal prison. Chuck was given a slightly longer sentence of five years because he had thrown the bank teller to the ground, injuring her.

When he got out of prison, Percy moved back to Australia. Reflecting on his crime in the *Australian Story* interview, Percy said, "We didn't really want to rob a bank. We were just talking about it and thinking about it and joking about how we could actually do it and then before we knew it, it just turned serious." He knows the robbery was foolish: "You'd have to be [stupid] to think you can get away with it."

BOND. JAIL BOND.

A British man wanted in Australia on "serious drug charges" was arrested by police in March 2019 while trying to flee the country on a jet ski.

The Australian Border Force in Bamaga, at the tip of Cape York, was tipped off that a man, "possibly armed with a crossbow and carrying additional fuel and supplies," had been seen launching the jet ski from Punsand Bay, on the northernmost edge of Queensland.

The fifty-seven-year-old suspect was wanted for alleged drug offenses in Western Australia. According to *The Guardian*, the man almost made it to Saibai Island, and was probably attempting to get all the way to Papua New Guinea. He was arrested on the mudflats on the eastern side of Saibai after traveling 93 miles across the Torres Strait.

"He gave it a red-hot go," said Jock O'Keeffe of the Queensland Police Service. O'Keeffe said the man was known to have had a crossbow on his journey, but didn't have it with him when he was arrested.

Citizens assisted the police in tracking the man through the Torres Strait Islands, notifying them when he had passed or landed on their islands, *The Guardian* reported.

"It's a bit unusual to try and get from Punsand Bay all the way to PNG. He stuck out like the proverbial," O'Keeffe said. But, he added, "We wouldn't have gone to this sort of effort if they weren't significant charges."

OVER THE HANDLEBARS

Between 1998 and 2002, Olympic-hopeful bike racer "Ted" robbed twenty-six banks in California, Illinois and Wisconsin. The FBI nicknamed him "the Choir Boy Robber" because he concealed his face from surveillance cameras by wearing a ball cap and bowing his head; also, he often held his hands together in front of him while at the counter.

Law enforcement was baffled by the Choir Boy's apparent lack of a getaway vehicle. Of course, that was because Ted biked to his bank heists. He'd leave his custom road bike outside, then enter the bank and hand the teller a note demanding the money and saying he had a gun. According to *Chicago* magazine, he would collect his loot and walk out of the bank, put the money in his messenger bag, strip down to the cycling clothes he was wearing under his street clothes and ride away, just another cyclist.

Ted started racing at the age of thirteen in his hometown of Libertyville, Illinois. He won his first race, at the local velodrome, and by high school was training almost every day. He was selected for the Olympic Training Camp in Colorado Springs as a high school junior and hoped to make the U.S. team after university. But he got through collegiate racing on talent, without putting in much training.

Ted had many ambitions. He wanted to become an emergency medical technician or join the French Foreign Legion. He tried several careers, including social worker, priest and underwater welder, but none of them satisfied him.

One other thing on his wish list was robbing a bank, so he decided to do that. However, as any good bank robber does, Ted didn't just fantasize about it, he made a plan and prepared his moves. He chose a Libertyville bank, picked a spot to stash his bike and rehearsed every step of the way. He ran through the trip in his mind, walking in place in his room. He turned his bookshelf into a teller's window and practiced pulling the note out of his pocket. His first heist, in 1998, went off without a hitch, and subsequent robberies were also success-ful. Until they weren't.

At first, Ted robbed banks for the pleasure of doing something really well. He gave away most of what he stole to homeless people or randomly to members of the public. He even threw cash into trash bins. But after he injured himself training for Olympic trials, he became addicted to painkillers and other drugs. As his addictions grew, money became more important to him, and he started to keep his ill-gotten gains.

The bicycle that served Ted so well was eventually his undoing. It was a custom-built orange Steelman racer that he'd bought second-hand. Steelman is a small company in Redwood City, California, that only makes about fifty bikes a year.

In March 2002, a police officer responding to a bank robbery in Walnut Creek, California, spotted a man in spandex cycling gear leaving the scene on an orange bike with a messenger bag. The suspicious officer flagged the cyclist down and asked to see inside his bag.

Ted raced away, and the policeman radioed for help, but the former elite cyclist managed to evade the police, ditching his bike and hiding out. Later, officers found the abandoned Steelman bike and Ted's cycling shoes.

The distinctive high-end bicycle eventually led the police to Ted, who was arrested in May 2002. He confessed, pleaded guilty and spent nine years in federal prison. At last report, he was working in a dough-nut shop and, at forty-eight, was still racing at the same Libertyville velodrome where he first fell in love with cycling.

DEFLATED

A Washington man who robbed a bank in Monroe almost made a clean getaway in his vehicle of choice: an inner tube.

"Austin" was the captain of his high school football and basketball teams, dated the cheerleading captain and went to college on a football scholarship. Then addiction to painkillers led him into a life of crime.

Austin played football at his father's alma mater, the University of Idaho, fulfilling his childhood dream. But while returning a punt in practice, Austin tore his anterior cruciate ligament, an injury that ended his promising football career and introduced him to the powerful painkiller Vicodin, according to *The Seattle Times*. Austin quickly became addicted to the prescription pills, once even going so far as to kick an oak coffee table repeatedly to injure himself so that he could obtain more pills.

Despite his painkiller habit, Austin was able to maintain the appearance of a successful business owner and family man. He graduated from college, married his high-school sweetheart, fathered two daughters and owned a real-estate investment company based in Seattle.

When he graduated from Vicodin to crack and benzodiazepines, Austin needed a way to fund the $15,000 a month he was spending on drugs. By his mid-twenties, he had organized several high-dollar thefts, scams and loan-sharking schemes, fenced stolen furniture and backed a sports-memorabilia counterfeiting ring.

But when the housing market collapsed, a desperate Austin decided he was going to rob a bank—and not for a mere few thousand dollars. Austin was meticulous in his planning. For three months, he observed a Brink's armored car as it made deliveries to the Bank of America branch in Monroe. He learned the schedule, diagrammed the locations of the bank's cameras and noted the armored car's blind spots.

In September 2008, a group of fifteen to twenty men showed up in the parking lot of the Monroe Bank of America. All but one of them were responding to a Craigslist ad that offered $28.50 an hour for work on a fictitious city cleanup project. They were told to show up at 11 a.m. wearing safety glasses, a ventilator mask, a yellow safety vest and a blue shirt.

At 11:05, just as a Brink's armored truck pulled up to the bank, one of the men sprinted across the road. It was Austin, armed with a can of mace. After taking out the security guard, Austin grabbed two bags of cash containing $400,000 and darted back through the parking lot, running past a bunch of men who looked just like him, which made eyewitness descriptions pretty much useless.

Next, Austin jumped into an inner tube he'd stashed by a nearby creek and, using prepared cables, pulled himself upstream about 200 yards to where his getaway car was stashed. After his months of careful planning, Austin had gotten away clean . . . or so he thought.

He'd made one mistake. A few weeks before the robbery, when Austin went to rehearse the heist, a homeless man spotted him acting suspiciously and took down his license plate number. The witness called the police after the robbery and told them what he had seen, and the police eventually matched Austin's DNA to a ventilator mask he'd left behind near the crime scene.

The inner-tube bandit spent five years in federal prison. He was released in April 2013 and returned to the Seattle area, where he reunited with his wife and daughters. He now writes children's books and is a public speaker about the dangers of drug abuse and how crime doesn't pay. He's an expert on both topics.

DRIVING MISS LAZY

In April 2018, Maryland detectives ended an armed robbery spree across central Baltimore County and the city of Baltimore that began and ended at a CVS drugstore.

The robberies were committed by a woman with teardrop tattoos on her face. But it wasn't the distinctive facial decorations that did her in—it was the fact that she didn't know how to drive a car.

According to a report from *CBS Baltimore*, "Kendra," thirty, was arrested while hiding behind a bus shelter after shoplifting at the same store where she had begun her robbery spree three months earlier. The arrest cleared that shoplifting case, four Baltimore County armed robbery cases and several others in the city of Baltimore.

Kendra was allegedly paying people to drive her to various stores, where she would commit the armed robberies by showing what appeared to be a handgun and demanding cash. She would then have the hired driver spirit her away.

But that day in April, she was confronted by a CVS employee as she placed items into a bag she was carrying. She pushed the employee aside and fled the store.

Her driver became suspicious when the employee followed Kendra out of the store, arguing with her as she got back in the car. The driver took Kendra across the street and told her to get out of the car. He then called the store, where police had just arrived on the scene, and told an officer what was going on.

Responding police officers saw Kendra trying to hide behind a nearby bus shelter and arrested her.

Kendra confessed to committing the crimes, blaming her drug addiction for the robberies. She was charged with armed robbery, assault and theft.

TECHNO-COLLAR

DON'T GO PRO

In the advanced modern age, it's hard to keep up to date. Two South African thieves were victims of the constant technological innovation when they attempted to rob a mountain biker, unaware that the biker's GoPro was filming them in high def.

A report by *The Citizen* reveals that cyclist "Maddox" was riding on a trail near the town of Somerset West in June 2014 when he took a wrong turn. A man flagged him down and, when Maddox stopped his bike, pulled a gun on him. Two other men ran up, and one of them frisked Maddox at knifepoint. The three robbers took Maddox's cell phone, Oakley sunglasses and mountain bike.

But after examining Maddox's GoPro closely, the robbers—who didn't seem to know what it was—decided they didn't want it. The camera was mounted on Maddox's helmet and, of course, recorded the entire crime.

Maddox took his camera footage to local police, who used the video to identify and arrest all three suspects. Police were also able to track down the stolen cell phone and bike. No word on the sunglasses.

STICKING IT TO THE MAN

Taunting law enforcement is almost never a good idea. If you need any proof of this, a perfect example happened in August 2018, when police in Seattle, Washington, were able to recapture a man who had escaped from King County Jail, thanks to the suspect's irresistible urge to insult a police detective.

KOMO News reported that, after breaking out, the escapee sent a text to a Seattle Police Major Crimes Task Force supervisor using a homophobic slur and telling him to perform a sex act.

Because the text message gave them the number of the cell phone used to send it, the supervisor and MCTF detectives were able to acquire a search warrant to obtain the phone data, which in turn led them to the suspect. While arresting him, police found that he was in possession of a small amount of methamphetamine, which they seized.

As a bonus, when a friend of the escapee came by to see how he was doing, detectives recognized him as a suspected burglar and placed him under arrest as well. This friend had a pellet pistol on him and was also carrying a small amount of methamphetamine.

Both men were booked into King County Jail on felony narcotics charges.

GPS (GLOBAL POSITIONING STUPIDITY)

It took a gang of armed robbers just ten seconds to storm a jewelry store and make off with £20,000 worth of gold jewelry. But as slick as the robbery was, the *Mirror* reported, "a catalogue of embarrassing errors" led police right to the gang's front door.

In November 2015, the staff of G. Naran Jewellers in Leicester, England, were subjected to terror when three masked men raided the store wielding axes. The store's security camera captured the men smashing glass cabinets and snatching items from the impressive collection of bracelets and rings. As the shop filled up with deterrent smoke, the video footage recorded the men fleeing the store and climbing into their getaway car, a stolen Nissan Qashqai.

While this plan seems foolproof enough, during the trial, the prosecution at Leicester Crown Court was quick to outline the mistakes that led police to the burglars. Not only were they sloppy enough to leave behind two of the axes, with the original price tags still attached, but they also neglected to erase the data on the GPS system of the getaway car. The axes were easily tracked back to the shop where they were purchased, connecting the men to the weapons. And upon recovering the getaway car, the police quickly realized that the inept criminals had used its GPS to navigate their way home, meaning the investigators could easily track where the men had taken the stolen goods.

Police also recovered a baseball cap and a mask near the scene of the crime that contained traces of one of the men's DNA.

The men were jailed for a combined total of twenty-one years.

After sentencing the trio, Judge Robert Brown said, "It was a carefully thought-out and a very determined robbery, even if in certain respects it was bungled. This was pre-planned and the car you used to come to Leicester in was stolen."

Prosecutor James Thomas noted, "This was a well-planned and professional robbery. None of the jewelry was recovered. Staff in the shop were very frightened and some screamed in fear. It's had a significant effect upon the victims."

Two of the criminals were only seventeen at the time of the break-in. The lawyer who defended the third perpetrator said, "He's slightly older but it appears they were youngsters trying to copy what would be a sophisticated robbery but failed hopelessly. The Qashqai car was left with the engine running, the doors wide open and a sat nav pinpointing where they'd come from. It was excruciatingly amateurish. The police couldn't believe their luck as they were given the address of my client so the defendants might as well have gone to the police station and handed themselves in."

Detective Chief Inspector Rich Ward explained, "Our inquiries quickly led us to Birmingham, where, with the assistance of West Midlands Police, we were able to arrest the suspects and charge them within a month of the incident. This was an extremely traumatic incident for those in the shop or who may have witnessed the activity. Incidents of this nature are rare in Leicester, but we're not complacent. We work closely with business owners in the Belgrave area to ensure their security is adequate and we meet with them on a regular basis to address any concerns."

THEY'RE TOASTED

Two overzealous burglars implicated themselves in a robbery when they recorded themselves drinking and spraying each other with stolen champagne.

According to the *Daily Mail*, the criminals stole almost £20,000 worth of goods from two homes in Birmingham, England, in December 2015. They took eight bottles of champagne, including a 2004 Taittinger and a rare 1973 Bollinger, from one of their targets on December 23. On December 19, they had knocked a man out and locked him in his flat before stealing £2,000 worth of belongings, including his car.

Police were able to track down the men a few days later, after the stolen car was spotted being driven the wrong way down a two-lane highway with its headlights off. "Kalim," the man driving the car, attempted to evade police by speeding up to 60 miles per hour down the highway. However, this was fruitless, as a police helicopter joined the chase and quickly located Kalim and the car in a parking lot.

After arresting Kalim and his accomplice, "Jaden," police were able to go through the two criminals' phones. Jaden's phone held a video of him making a toast with the stolen champagne and a photo of him wearing a stolen watch.

Both men admitted two counts of burglary at Birmingham Crown Court in May 2016.

Kalim was given five years and two months behind bars and banned from the roads for four years and two months. Jaden was jailed for five years.

"The files on Jaden's phone were damning," the detective constable said. "He is shown posing with the bottles just minutes after the burglary and then opening them during a Christmas party. He refused to answer any questions during the interview, and Kalim initially denied being involved at all. However, we secured compelling evidence against the pair and they were left with little choice but to admit their guilt."

THIS DOESN'T COMPUTE

On September 18, 2006, thirty-nine-year-old "Jim" pleaded guilty to charges of computer theft. He would have had a hard time denying the charges, since he had been caught in the act of stealing six computers from the courthouse after his trial for other computer-theft charges.

Jim and a friend had attempted to steal computer equipment from a publishing business in Ignacio, California, but were caught when alarms went off. Jim's hearing on these charges, at the Novato Civic Center in Novato, California, was held on September 13 of that year. After the hearing, Jim hid in the courthouse until everyone had gone home, then stole six computers and their monitors, rolling them out of the building in a recycling bin. According to police, he was actually stopped by sheriff's deputies and maintenance workers as he was attempting to leave, but since no one could prove he'd stolen the computers, they let him go.

The next morning, when officials at the courthouse realized they were missing six computers, all police investigators had to do was review the surveillance camera tapes, which gave them a clear view of Jim at work.

Incredibly, Jim was easy to find because he had been arrested later that same night trying to steal a Volkswagen in nearby San Rafael.

According to the Associated Press, Jim faced new charges that included attempted auto theft, burglary and grand theft. He pleaded guilty to them all.

Sheriff's Sergeant Jerry Niess said, "It just amazed me that someone could be in the middle of a jury trial for a burglary involving computers and immediately get involved in another burglary at the Civic Center."

Jim explained to reporters at the county jail that he had stolen the computers "for personal reasons." "I needed help," Jim said, "and I didn't know how to ask for help. And I guess, in my crazy way, this was my way of asking for help."

He continued, "A lot of things are going crazy in my life. I was losing control. It probably doesn't make a good story, but it's the truth."

In our opinion, it's a pretty good story.

PIKACHU!

When the augmented reality game Pokémon Go was released on July 6, 2016, it became an immediate hit around the world, with millions of players using their mobile phones to track and capture imaginary creatures superimposed onto the real world.

The game features technicolor cartoon animals that could hardly look more innocent or fun. Unfortunately, within just a few days, criminals in O'Fallon, Missouri, figured out a way to turn the game from treasure hunt into armed robbery, luring players to secluded locations and holding them up at gunpoint.

As Sergeant Bill Stringer of the O'Fallon Police Department told *The Guardian*, "Using the geolocation feature, the robbers were able to anticipate the location and level of seclusion of unwitting victims." Another spokesperson added: "You can add a beacon to a pokestop to lure more players."

Thankfully, these four bandits, suspects in a string of robberies, were apprehended relatively quickly in the parking lot of a CVS pharmacy by police officers responding to a report of armed robbery. One officer observed the suspects trying to get rid of a handgun, throwing it out of the car as the police approached.

The suspects ranged in age from sixteen to eighteen, and the adults among them were charged with first-degree robbery and had bail set at $100,000.

In a Facebook post, the O'Fallon Police Department issued an advisory to the public: "If you use this app (or other similar-type apps) or have children that do, we ask you to please use caution when alerting strangers of your future location."

Niantic, the developer of Pokémon Go, cautions players to

maintain a safe level of awareness while tracking Pokémon creatures, staying grounded in the real world even as they hunt for treasure in the augmented world. Police and state agencies have also spoken up, warning people not to break the law in their pursuits, and not to enter into situations or areas where they might put themselves in danger.

But despite this sound advice, some players have already been injured while playing the game, and one unlucky nineteen-year-old Wyoming resident discovered a real-life corpse, believed to be an accidental death.

OMG, DELETE THAT!

When "Daniel" saw the unflattering mug shot the police had posted of him, he knew he couldn't take it lying down.

According to the BBC, in an interview with a local radio station, Daniel stressed his case: "Man, they just did me wrong. They put a picture out that made me look like I was a Thundercat . . . or James Brown on the run. I can't do that."

So he did something about it. In 2015 Daniel sent the police a photo that, in his opinion, was more flattering, texting: "Here is a better photo that one is terrible."

The Lima Police Department in Ohio updated their Facebook post, which had asked the public to help them locate the suspected arsonist, writing: "This photo was sent to us by [Daniel] himself. We thank him for being helpful, but now we would appreciate it if he would come to speak to us at the LPD about his charges."

Daniel was arrested in 2016 in Florida, CNN reported.

CALLING IT IN

It's hard to imagine just what was going through "Billy's" head when he pinched his own defense lawyer's cell phone—during a court hearing, no less.

In June 2016, Camberwell Green Magistrates' Court in London, England, heard how Billy, twenty-six, had in May of the previous year pleaded guilty to possession of cannabis and driving without insurance, was ordered to pay a fine and court costs, and had six points put on his driving license.

Following the case, he had a meeting with his lawyer to talk about how he would pay his fines. *The Sun* reported that she turned away from Billy for a moment, giving him the irresistible opportunity to grab her £300 Samsung Galaxy phone.

After leaving the courtroom, the lawyer realized her phone was missing and reported it stolen to the police. When looking through the CCTV footage from the courtroom, Police Constable David Paine could easily make out Billy stealing the phone.

Unsurprisingly, Billy was arrested and charged with theft. He had another fourteen days added to a jail sentence he previously received for a different offense and was ordered to pay an £80 victim surcharge.

After Billy was found guilty, PC Paine said, "I'm pleased with the conviction. [Billy] is a repeat offender. This crime shows he doesn't care who he targets or what misery he causes."

THEY GOT SHOPPED

COME BACK LATER

A quick-thinking shopkeeper in Charleroi, Belgium, told a band of armed robbers that he didn't have much money in the till and they should "come back later." Amazingly, the robbers were just dumb enough for this ruse to work.

The *Daily Mail* reported that the owner of the e-cigarette shop, who identified himself as Didier, said six armed men entered his store at 3 p.m. one Saturday in October 2018 and ordered him to hand over all his money. Didier suggested they return in a few hours, when there would be more money in the cash register.

"I told them that 3 p.m. is not the best time to hold up a store," Didier said, adding that he advised them, "You'll take 1,000 euros, but if you come back tonight you might be able to take 2,000 or 3,000."

Incredibly, the robbers left, saying they would be back. ("They weren't the brightest," Didier said.) The vape shop owner contacted the police, who understandably didn't believe the gang would return and declined to wait for them.

Despite the police skepticism, the would-be robbers returned at 5:30 p.m. Didier gave them hell for arriving before closing time: "'You have to buy a watch,' I said. 'It's 5:30, not 6:30,' and they left."

The six bandits—the gang who couldn't think straight?—did as they were told, and this time, when they returned, undercover police officers were waiting to arrest them.

"It's like it was a comedy," Didier told the BBC. "They're being called the worst robbers in Belgium."

Belgian broadcaster RTL reported that five members of the group were arrested, including one minor, while the sixth offender fled the scene.

NO HONOR AMONG DUMB CRIMINALS

The saying "what goes around comes around" proved to be only too true for a Utah couple.

A thirty-six-year-old man and a forty-six-year-old woman from Ogden, Utah, were caught shoplifting one afternoon in December 2011, at a WinCo Foods grocery store. While they were being questioned inside the store, a thief broke into their truck in the parking lot and proceeded to rob them, taking a stereo, an amplifier, a drum machine and cigarettes.

According to *Deseret News*, the couple took about $50 worth of makeup, energy bars and batteries from the store. The guy who broke into their truck took items worth about $150.

"Store security had the individuals in custody, in their office," said Ogden Police Lieutenant Eric Young. "They had reviewed surveillance video and recovered stolen property from the suspects." The couple were cited for shoplifting and released by the investigating officer.

As the officer left the store, he saw the two shoplifters "trying to flag him down in the parking lot," Young said. They told him their truck had been broken into and robbed.

Police have security footage of the car burglar in action, from the same surveillance system that caught the alleged shoplifters. The video shows a man in a red sweater checking out the truck and eventually breaking in.

"I think they were unlucky," Young said. "This is something that happened. I guess it wasn't dark, but it was starting to get dark."

Police say they don't usually hear of car burglaries at that shopping center. Sounds like it really was karma. And, as we all know, karma can be a botch.

POINTING THE FINGER

A man in Florida attempted to rob two convenience stores wielding nothing but a finger gun. Yes, you read that right.

The nineteen-year-old wannabe robber pulled his stunt one night in February 2008, pointing his finger gun at the clerk behind the counter at a Circle K store in Daytona Beach and demanding the cash from the register.

As reported by the news site Metro, the clerk, understandably, assumed it was some sort of prank. Even when he realized the robber was, in fact, serious, there was little reason for him to feel alarmed: finger guns don't shoot bullets. He confronted the robber, who fled.

The man then met up with a friend, and the pair entered a 7-Eleven store in the same neighborhood. This time, the men, still wielding only finger weapons, were more successful, getting away with $41, some cigarettes and a twelve-pack of beer. However, later that night police tracked them down, along with their stolen goods.

Both men were charged with robbery, and the original finger-pointer faced an additional attempted robbery charge.

FALLING DOWN ON THE JOB

Everything about this 2018 botched robbery was a mess. Everything. Security camera footage released by police shows a man walking into an Aurora, Colorado, e-cigarette store and trying to take out a handgun, which police later said was a BB pistol. Astoundingly, the man lost his grip and the gun flew over the counter.

"The BB gun, with the orange tip removed, fell onto the floor where the clerk grabs it," the Aurora Police Department said in a Facebook post.

The video, posted by *Global News*, captures the look of surprise on the suspect's face as the gun sailed across the counter. He started to climb over the counter himself, but changed his mind and ran out the door.

In one last moment of utter humiliation, the video shows the man losing his pants before running out of sight. It's safe to say he won't be showing his face in that store again.

THICK AS A BRICK

A Maryland man was given the appropriate name "Bad Luck Bandit" after he hit himself in the head with a brick he threw at a window.

According to the Prince George's County Police Department, the man was caught on surveillance video breaking into a store in September 2018. He shattered the front window with a brick, walked in and then tried to use the same brick to break the window protecting the front counter.

Turns out the second window was made of bulletproof glass. But the man was nothing if not persistent in his endeavor to break it. Unfortunately, on his third try, the brick ricocheted off the window and hit him in the head, knocking him down. The Associated Press reported that he lay there for a few minutes before getting up and fleeing the scene.

BONG!

Three men armed with bear spray attempted to rob a marijuana dispensary in Shannonville, Ontario, but were fought off by one of the shop's clerks, who used the only weapon he had on hand: a bong.

There were four criminals altogether, police said. According to *CBC News*, one of them waited in the getaway car—a white Mazda SUV—while the other three attempted to rob the Recreational Cannabis Farmers Market on Old Highway 2 in September 2018.

The Tyendinaga Police Service said the three would-be robbers entered the dispensary with their faces covered and squirted the two clerks with what looked like pepper spray. One of the clerks wouldn't give up, though, and fought the men off, swinging a large glass pipe at them until they fled.

The four suspects were last seen driving away from the scene and have not been captured.

It's not the first time dispensaries in the area have been targeted. "This would be our second robbery in the past two weeks," Detective Constable Nathan Leland said.

BUT FIRST, A DRINK

MAGNUM CUM LAUDE

A man who broke into a wealthy financier's Hong Kong home had to be rescued from a hillside after twisting his ankle while fleeing police.

The twenty-two-year-old undocumented immigrant, who, according to police, had been squatting in an empty house in Hong Kong's exclusive Peak area, stole items valued at $120,000 from the home of businessman "Leo" in December 1997.

He had also broken into the neighboring home of Goldman Sachs Asia managing director "Hugh," who was in New York on a business trip. Once in the house, the man downed a bottle of Moët & Chandon and a can of Diet Coke. He then raided Hugh's fridge, helping himself to leftover rice with fish sauce and chiles.

His stomach now full, but unable to resist such a well-stocked fridge, the man packed himself a snack for later: a box of rice, some noodles, lettuce and a bottle of cooking oil. He also added some coins to his bounty. There is such a detailed record of the burglar's loot because, perhaps giddy from the bubbles, he forgot the bag containing the coins and his food, leaving it at Hugh's. The only objects he remembered to take with him were two kitchen knives, which he later dropped in Leo's home, connecting him to both break-ins.

The *South China Morning Post* reported that Hugh's maid slept through the break-in.

A BUBBLY PERSONALITY

In October 2014, French police in the historic town of Provins, just outside Paris, caught a burglar drunk on champagne, sprawled in the front of the television in the house he was robbing.

When the owners returned from an evening out, they noted that the house looked like it had been broken into and decided to stay outside and call the police.

According to the English-language French news site *The Local*, the man offered no resistance when the officers entered. "He was just sitting there in front of the television with a bottle of champagne, almost empty," a police source said. "It was one in the morning and he was very relaxed, completely intoxicated, and had apparently forgotten where he was."

The forty-two-year-old man was arrested in possession of cash, a passport and a pair of sunglasses that he had stolen from the house. He had also taken out a bicycle on which to make a getaway, although police commented that they suspected the man was too drunk to ride it.

Shockingly, it seems that it is quite common for burglaries to be foiled by champagne consumption. A homeowner in Esperance, Western Australia, had little to celebrate when she returned home to find a man asleep in her bed after he had helped himself to her champagne. The thirty-six-year-old man had apparently kicked down the door to her home in an attempt to rob her, but his plan changed when he found a bottle of Louis Perdrier Brut Excellence, *The Sacramento Bee* reported.

"He has consumed some champagne," said investigating police officer Richard Moore. "It must have been quite potent because he fell asleep in the resident's bed, which is not a good thing, and the owner has returned home and located this male person in her bed."

The Louis Perdrier champagne sells for about $13 a bottle in Australia, which doesn't seem worth going to jail for.

When tested by police, the man proved to be highly intoxicated, with a blood alcohol level more than eight times the legal driving limit. As a precaution, the police took him to the hospital after his arrest.

BRUT WEAKNESS

In September 2018, citizens in Dusseldorf, Germany, were concerned to see a man parked on the side of the road, seemingly unconscious in the front seat of his car, and alerted authorities. According to a report by *IOL*, the man had recently stolen money and jewelry, as well as a bottle of champagne that he was eager to consume—so eager, in fact, that he botched his getaway. When the officers who arrived at the scene woke the man from his champagne-induced snooze and asked for his ID, they quickly realized he was wanted for several robberies.

"The officers couldn't believe their luck when they found out who he was," a police spokesperson said. "He even had the stolen goods from his latest robbery with him in the car. And we got him for drunk driving as well."

He may not have been smart, but at least he had a strong sense of occasion.

THE CASE OF THE STOLEN CHAMPAGNE

A fifty-year-old man was sentenced to twenty months in jail after using a James Bond technique to steal champagne. Instead of breaking a window or cracking a lock, as other thieves tend to do, he used a rope to descend into a London theater to steal thirty-two bottles of champagne, the *Evening Standard* reported.

In January 2018, the suspect entered the New London Theatre in Drury Lane (now called the Gillian Lynne Theatre), which is said to be adjacent to the apartment building where he lived. He was subsequently spotted on CCTV carrying the champagne, disguised in bins, out the stage door.

In April, he broke into the Bunga Bunga bar and pizzeria, also in Drury Lane, and was caught on camera making off with vodka.

The drink thief, who had fifty-four previous convictions, was sentenced in May at Blackfriars Crown Court after pleading guilty to both offenses, as well as the robbery of a dental surgery.

ALCOHOLICS NOTORIOUS

A woman who drove drunk on her way to an Alcoholics Anonymous meeting got pretty much what she had coming after she hit and seriously injured a student, then crashed her car into the church where the AA meeting was to be held.

Police said "Breana," seventy-three, of Boulder, Colorado, was drunk when, in October 2012, she clipped the Cheese Louise food truck parked in the church parking lot before hitting the victim, an eighteen-year-old University of Colorado freshman, while he was sitting at a nearby table, eating lunch. The SUV then crashed into the church's covered entryway.

The student was thrown about 30 feet and ended up at Boulder Community Hospital in serious condition, with a punctured lung and several broken ribs. Breana was not injured.

Fox31 Denver reported that there were about twenty people in the vicinity of the food truck outside St. Aidan's Episcopal Church when Breana appeared on the scene. The food truck owner said he saw her SUV "take out the table right behind me," and added that his truck "shook like an earthquake" from the impact of the crash.

Breana, who failed a sobriety test on the scene, said she was on her way to an Alcoholics Anonymous meeting in St. Aidan's hall.

Breana initially pleaded not guilty to one count of vehicular assault (a felony) and two misdemeanor counts of driving under the influence, but changed her plea to guilty on all three charges. If convicted after pleading not guilty, she could have received two to six years in prison for the vehicular assault charge. Instead, she was sentenced to sixty days in jail and five days' probation.

AND THAT'S THE TOOTH

"Jeffrey," a thirty-eight-year-old British man, broke into a garage looking for items he could steal. But, as the *Huddersfield Daily Examiner* reported, what he found was some beer and a freezer full of Popsicles. So he did what any mastermind criminal would do: he took out his dentures and sat back to enjoy Popsicles and beer. He enjoyed himself so much that, after indulging in the treats, he forgot to put his teeth back in, leaving them behind for the owner to find. The choppers were discovered by Steven Pickles, fifty-eight, who found them near the freezer a few days later.

Jeffrey, who had already been arrested for several other burglaries, was easily tracked down using the abandoned dentures.

Pickles told the *Examiner*, "The garage wasn't locked, so he had sneaked in and helped himself to the beer. I reported it to police at the time, and a few days later I went in the garage and found a set of false teeth down the side of the freezer. I moved them to a shelf, then told the police."

Jeffrey already had a criminal record, having previously been charged for an attempted robbery in which he disturbed a sleeping pensioner and was subsequently chased away by the pensioner's adept use of his walking stick.

The court heard that Jeffrey was a heroin addict, and that he had been searching for items he could sell to sustain his habit. Because of his drunken condition, his lawyer said, Jeffrey had only a hazy recollection of the events in the garage.

He was jailed for sixteen months at Leeds Crown Court.

ROCK, PAPER, FREEDOM

It's something you don't see every day.

The occasion was Chilifest, a country music festival outside College Station, Texas, in April 2015. A young girl took on a police officer in a game of rock-paper-scissors to decide whether she'd be ticketed for underage drinking. Win, and she would walk free. Lose, and she would be subject to a court appearance, fines, a criminal record, compulsory classes and—not least—removal from the festival, as reported by the *Daily Mail*.

She threw a rock. The officer showed scissors.

A video posted by an onlooker revealed the girl's delight as her friends hugged her in congratulations. The cop and two other officers left the scene.

However, *KBTX-TV* reported, as good as the incident was for community relations, the policemen's superiors were not amused. The three officers were banned from working future Chilifests and were subject to further discipline from their departments.

LEAVE ME YOUR CARD

LICENSE TO NIL

In June 2018, a robber walked into a Huntington Bank branch in Columbus, Ohio, and gave the teller a note demanding money and revealing that he had a gun. The teller gave the man a stack of cash, but that wasn't enough for him. He told the teller to get him more money from the cash recycler in the bank's lobby. According to police, the quick-thinking teller told the robber the machine wouldn't dispense cash without a driver's license. Unbelievably, the robber handed his ID over.

The license, of course, led police directly to the fifty-one-year-old man, who was arrested and charged with aggravated robbery and threatening with a deadly weapon.

NOW YOU CV, NOW YOU DON'T

A gambling addict held up a betting shop in Birmingham, England, at gunpoint and made off with over £17,000.

Sounds like a pretty well-planned heist, no? It probably would have been, if it weren't for the fact that the robber, "Amir," had left his résumé at the very same shop. You know, that document that contains, among other personal details, your contact information?

Unsurprisingly, Amir was rapidly captured.

According to *BirminghamLive*, Amir, twenty-six, walked into the bookie's place at 8:25 a.m. one day in March 2017 wearing a hood and a mask. He walked up to the counter and revealed a gun. Police later recovered a betting slip on which he had written, "I got a gun, open the door or I'll shoot you." He forced the assistant manager to open the safe and fill a carrier bag with £16,700 in notes and £360 in coins, plus another £200 taken from the till.

So far, the heist was going well. But then Amir made a fatal mistake. As he was leaving, he removed his mask, and a security camera got a clear picture of his partly covered face. The store manager later identified him as a customer who had been in the shop several times. He had been looking for work and had provided his CV. And the manager still had it.

Thanks to the very helpful CV, police were easily able to identify Amir as the robber, said prosecutor Rob Cowley.

After searching Amir's home, police recovered a simulated firearm, the threatening note and the carrier bag.

Cowley said Amir had also been present when another man, "Hamza," used the same fake weapon to try to rob a betting shop in Washwood Heath in April. That robbery was foiled, however, when the manager of the shop activated the alarm that filled the store with deterrent smoke. Police quickly arrived and Hamza was arrested. Hamza was sentenced to three years and four months after pleading guilty to attempted robbery and possessing an imitation firearm and a knife.

As his punishment for the Birmingham heist, Amir, who had previously admitted robbery and possessing an imitation firearm, was jailed for six years.

Amir's defense counsel said, "[Amir] had a longstanding gambling addiction which had been going on for three or four years. He had developed an obsession with online gambling." The lawyer disclosed that Amir had run up a £22,000 debt with one firm of bookies over an eleven-month period, and owed £2,000 to another.

CASH GRAB

A man walked into a Bank of America in San Gabriel, California, in March 2018 to complain that the ATM outside wouldn't give him any cash. Frustrated with the bank and the broken machine, he started shouting at a teller and grabbed some of the money she was counting. She fought him for the bills, and after a struggle, he ran off with about $20.

But according to the *Pasadena Star-News*, he left behind his ID and ATM cards, which gave police all the information they needed to track him down. The crime was considered a robbery, even though the man thought he was owed the money, because he used force to take it.

WE'RE IN YOUR DEBIT

"Alan," fifty-six, entered a branch of the Wells Fargo bank in San Diego, California, one morning in May 2017. Dressed in a distinctive black-and-white-checked coat, Alan walked to a teller's desk and swiped his Wells Fargo debit card, providing the teller with his account information, according to *Fox 5*.

Alan admitted in court that he demanded cash from the teller, saying, "You're being robbed. Don't make a mistake. . . . You don't want anyone to get hurt; don't make a mistake." He also handed the teller a note saying essentially the same thing. He made his getaway with $565.

Based on the information from Alan's customer profile, which was easily accessed thanks to his use of his own debit card, FBI agents and police detectives were able to quickly arrest him.

He could have been given a maximum sentence of twenty years, according to the U.S. Attorney's Office in San Diego. Instead, U.S. District Judge Anthony Battaglia gave him a forty-six-month jail sentence and ordered him to pay restitution of $565, the amount he had stolen.

ISSUES WITH MANAGEMENT

A St. Paul, Minnesota, man was accused of becoming angry and striking a woman while on his way to anger management class.

"Joshua," twenty-seven, pleaded guilty to fifth-degree assault in February 2008 and was sentenced to serve at least 120 days in jail, the county attorney's office said.

Fox News reported that in August 2007, Joshua was waiting at a bus stop one day at around 5 p.m. when he assaulted a fifty-nine-year-old woman and other people at the stop. "Why don't you show me some respect?" he shouted at the woman. When she attempted to call the police, Joshua hit her in the face.

When a sixty-three-year-old man tried to stop Joshua, Joshua hit him with a blue folder, which he then dropped when he decided to flee the scene. The folder, which contained Joshua's homework from his anger management class as well as his personal information, was all police needed to track him down.

COUNTING CHICKENS

A bank robber in Alaska could not wait to find out how much loot he had stolen. He was so excited, he couldn't even manage a proper getaway. Instead, he counted the money right outside the bank. Spoiler alert: he'd only managed to steal $400.

The *New York Post* reported that a man was taken into custody by police in Anchorage soon after leaving First National Bank Alaska.

"It's my understanding he was sitting outside the bank counting his money when police arrived," an FBI spokeswoman said.

Documents filed in U.S. District Court in Anchorage revealed that the suspect had entered the bank wearing a large backpack at about 4 p.m. on a Tuesday. He gave the teller a note reading "This is a hold up. Please put the money they want in the bag. God help us!!!"

According to the *Anchorage Daily News*, the would-be robber had written the note on the back of his housing application, which of course, had a lot of his personal information on it, including his name and birth date.

Inevitably, he confessed to the robbery.

CARDED

It's right there in the shoplifter's handbook: Don't leave your name and address in the shop you're lifting from. Also, don't brag about your shoplifting afterward on social media.

"Michael" obviously hadn't read the book.

To start with, Michael was caught on surveillance video at a consignment shop in Albuquerque, New Mexico, stealing a necklace in November 2016.

According to *Global News*, Michael, forty, was apprehended by police because, after the theft, he flirted with the clerk at the store and, when he couldn't immediately get a date, gave her his business card with all his contact information on it.

Looking at the surveillance video later, the clerk recognized Michael and handed his card to the police, who went onto Michael's Facebook timeline and found a video, uploaded from his car just after he left the consignment shop, in which he showed off the necklace and bragged about stealing it.

In the video, Michael said: "Pampering my perfectly porcelain princess with the gorgeous curves today. Raided a thrift store today for this necklace! I adore you, Emily (I call her my tipsy gypsy—she's got lots of cool kitschy gypsy jewelry). Upgrade."

"This guy's a goofball," an Albuquerque Police Department public information officer said. "I can't believe it. Well, I guess I can believe it. These guys are dumb. We didn't have to call Columbo in on this one, because this guy left his name with his business card after he shoplifted, trying to pick up the girl he shoplifted from."

The owner of the consignment shop where the necklace was

stolen said, "We looked him up on Facebook and, sure enough, he had posted the stolen necklace an hour or two later."

As it turned out, Michael posted often about items he had "raided." The Albuquerque Police Department revealed that Michael had outstanding warrants for shoplifting and theft in three other New Mexico jurisdictions.

So Albuquerque officers arrested and charged him a fourth time, and had a message for business owners in the area: "If this guy walks into your business, know that he's not there to purchase stuff, he's there to rip you off."

I'LL CATCH ME
IF YOU CAN'T

SNOWY DEMISE

The job of the police was made incredibly easy when, while attempting to track down a carjacker, all they had to do was follow a trail of footprints left in the snow. According to *NBC 4 New York*, the victim, who remained unidentified, told police that, upon seeing his car being stolen, he jumped into a company car and pursued the suspect. During the chase, the suspect crashed the stolen vehicle and, in a panic, attempted to flee on foot. Unfortunately for the twenty-three-year-old suspect, the freshly fallen snow meant that his path away from the car was immediately obvious to the responding officers. Police followed the footprints and quickly caught up with the suspect, who was charged with motor vehicle theft and resisting arrest.

HE COULD USE THE MONEY

"Ahmed," described by *BBC News* as a mid- or low-level Taliban commander in eastern Afghanistan's Paktika province, walked up to a police checkpoint in April 2012. Baffling the officers, he pointed to a wanted poster with a picture of his face on it, as well as his fingerprint and other information about him, and asked for the $100 bounty the poster was offering.

Ahmed, who was wanted for plotting at least two attacks with improvised explosive devices on U.S. and Afghan troops, was in for a disappointing surprise. Instead of giving him money, the soldiers arrested him.

Officials were so shocked by the incident that they gave the man in custody a biometric scan to prove that he was actually the suspected terrorist he claimed to be.

NATO, under U.S. command, had been increasing its presence in Paktika because it contained infiltration routes to the Afghan capital, Kabul, from Pakistan. They had tried using wanted posters before, but with little success.

One U.S. official called Ahmed "the Taliban equivalent of the *Home Alone* burglars." Another said, "Clearly, this man is an imbecile."

The *BBC News* report said Ahmed is not believed to have commanded many insurgents. It's easy to see why.

ON THE FENCE

A security camera in Kaulille, Belgium, recorded a comical sight in December 2018. The footage showed a thief stacking empty bread shelves in the loading area of a supermarket in an attempt to crawl over a nearby fence with a case of energy drinks.

The thief didn't make it very far, however, as his pants got caught on the fence's spikes. He proceeded to hang there upside down for hours, until some kind people passing by helped him down.

Supermarket owner Jos Craeghs told the Belgian newspaper *HLN* that the thief got stuck at 3 a.m. Once he was freed, he left the scene with twenty-four cans of Monster energy drink. Amazingly, the ambitious thief then returned at 5 a.m. to steal again. Craeghs said, "He again climbed over the fence and tried to steal a crate of Duvel [beer].

Again, he got stuck on the gate while trying to climb back outside. He tried to free himself by taking his pants off, but that did not work."

According to *HLN*, at around 6:30 a.m., people passing by spotted the thief, and this time they called police, who arrested him. The stolen beers and energy drinks were returned to the supermarket.

Craeghs said the police called him about the incident at 9 a.m. "We then went together to look at the CCTV footage. We almost rolled on the floor laughing."

The thirty-year-old thief, who could not be named for legal reasons, was known to police.

IT'S A LOCK

A man in Pretoria, South Africa, was arrested after the auto-lock system of the car he broke into self-activated and trapped him inside.

The South African news source *IOL* reported that the man used a jamming device to get into the vehicle. "I just saw him getting into the car after the woman walked away," a witness says. "It seems the doors locked him inside and he couldn't get out."

Panicking, the man shouted for help, claiming to be one of Pretoria's car guards. Amused passersby gathered and laughed. The police were called, but the man was stuck inside the car for nearly two hours before the owner returned to unlock it.

The owner of the car was shocked to return to her parked vehicle and find a man inside. According to *IOL*, she shouted "What are you doing in my car?" before unlocking it and letting the man out. The police were already on the scene and promptly arrested the suspect.

CLINGING TO HIS STORY

Scaling a tall building is no small feat, and most would agree that it's best to not attempt it at all unless you are Spider-Man or some other kind of professional.

This obvious truth did not stop one man. In April 2011, the *Daily News* reported on a burglary gone wrong in Anshan, China, where police found a man dangling from a fifth-story window. Officials suspected that he had scaled the wall of the apartment building in an attempt to break in, but got stuck. The terrified man was found clinging to the outside of an apartment block and ended up having to be rescued by police and firefighters. After a half-hour rescue effort, the thief was safely taken into custody.

HE SHOULDN'T HAVE DUCT

Everyone has days when everything goes wrong.

A man in Seattle, Washington, had one of those days in February 2015. All he wanted to do was steal some quarters from a soda machine in the laundry room of an apartment building, but his simple task turned into a comedy of errors.

According to *KIRO 7*, police were called when residents reported hearing what sounded like a person "destroying washing machines" in the laundry room. Knowing he had been caught, the thief blocked the door to the room and tried to escape by bashing through the drywall with his crowbar. He gave up on that when he ran into a proper masonry wall.

As building resident TJ Davis told *KIRO 7*, "The basement's all stone and rock and so he was kind of done going through walls at that point."

Realizing that he couldn't break through the walls, the burglar decided to try to escape through an air duct, a feat that looks simple enough in the movies. As you might expect, he got stuck and needed to be rescued by firefighters, who had to cut him free from the duct. To add insult to injury, residents videotaped his attempts to escape.

When the firefighters asked if he needed medical attention, he said, "Heroin."

THE FRYERS CLUB

A man who broke into a pizza restaurant in Rotterdam, New York, near Albany, ended up having to beg police to rescue him after he got himself wedged in an exhaust vent over the kitchen's hot fryer.

John Risko, the manager of Paesan's Pizza, found the grease-covered "Anthony" when he responded to a fire alarm late one night in March 2011. Risko told the *Daily Mail* that his boss had called to ask him to check out the alarm. When Risko reached the restaurant, instead of a fire, he found Anthony, stuck inside the vent.

"I come in, turn off the alarms, take a peek into the kitchen and see this guy's legs dangling out of the hood over the stove in the kitchen," Risko said.

As reported by the *Daily Mail*, Anthony had climbed a tree to get onto the roof, then used a hammer to gain access to the air duct. He became stuck when trying to slither down into the kitchen.

A spokesman for the Rotterdam Police, Lieutenant Michael Brown, said, "He became extremely distraught when he realized he was stuck over the fryer. He said he thought he was going to die. The fryer had been used all day, so it may have been generating some heat."

It took police thirty minutes to free Anthony from the shaft and take him into custody, Brown said. In his mug shot, Anthony's face, white T-shirt and jeans are coated in grease.

Risko said, "I just started laughing. Who would ever think of trying to do this? It's something you'd only see on TV."

The owner of Paesan's, Lorenzo Scavio, said in an interview with *Fox News*, "As he was coming down the hood, when he got to the bottom, he stepped on one of the pipes. The pipes burst, which triggered the alarm. These are tied to the fire-suppression system over the stove and fryers, and when it went off, it sent a blast of flame retardant through the kitchen. He was actually lucky that he tripped the fire system. If he didn't, he would have probably died in there.

"I think he's out of his mind. It doesn't make any sense. We don't keep any money in the store and you can't pull the equipment out. What was he trying to rob? It just doesn't make sense at all."

Schenectady's *Daily Gazette* reported that Anthony was arraigned on charges of burglary, criminal mischief and possession of burglary tools, and was taken to Schenectady County Jail. At his trial in 2013, prosecutors cited twenty-two small-business burglaries committed by Anthony since 1992. He had spent fourteen of the years in between in prison. His history made him eligible for a sentence of twenty-five years to life had the judge found him to be a persistent felon.

The judge chose the lesser punishment of three-and-a-half to seven years when sentencing Anthony, saying that the minimum under the persistent felony provision—fifteen years to life—was too great, and called on the New York state legislature to give judges more flexibility in sentencing persistent nonviolent offenders.

Anthony was released in July 2017, after about six years in custody, but was rearrested in 2018 for another restaurant break-in, this time through an unlocked window.

HE GOT THE CHAIR

An English man stealing lead from the roof of a 600-year-old heritage building ended up in a wheelchair after slipping and falling from atop the Tudor house.

Police found a twenty-year-old man in agony on the ground outside Birmingham's St. Nicolas Place complex early one morning in October 2015, *ITV News* reported. He had stolen lead worth £2,000 from the fifteenth-century Merchant's House, part of St. Nicolas Place, which was restored in 2004 when it was the winner of the BBC's program *Restoration*, in which viewers voted on which listed building would win a grant from the Heritage Lottery Fund.

According to *ITV News*, thieves had repeatedly stripped metal from the Merchant's House's roof over the years, causing damage of as much as £100,000.

In a trial a year after the robbery, prosecutor Gurpreet Sandhu told the Birmingham Crown Court, "Tudor Merchant's House . . . has been the subject of a great deal of investment, some of which has been widely publicized. . . . Tens of thousands of pounds of damage has been done to it." Sandhu said there could be no insurance claim because of all the previous thefts.

Sandhu told the court that police called to the scene found the stolen lead in a nearby parking lot. One of the thieves was found hiding behind bushes, and the twenty-year-old was discovered lying in the courtyard with a dislocated shoulder and damaged vertebrae, injuries that left him temporarily wheelchair-bound. He told police that he had stolen the metal because he needed money to repay debts.

Having already confessed to charges of theft and possessing an offensive weapon, he was sentenced to up to twenty-one months in jail.

"TRAPPED"

A man and a woman who believed they were trapped in a Daytona State College janitor's closet were rescued two days later by police, only to realize the door had never been locked. In fact, it didn't even have a lock.

As reported by the *Orlando Sentinel,* a thirty-one-year-old man and a twenty-five-year-old woman claimed they had been chased into the closet in the Marine and Environmental Science Center on December 28, 2014, while the college was closed for the holidays.

After two days in the closet, the man called 911 from his cell phone, police said. Officers tracked the phone's location and let the couple out.

It's unclear why the pair waited two days before calling 911, or what efforts they had made to escape their self-imposed "prison." When police went inside the closet and closed the door, they opened it easily from within and couldn't find a way to make it lock.

Inside the closet, police found copper scouring pads, which can be used to smoke crack cocaine, as well as human feces. They did not find any drugs.

A BUM RAP

GOLD MINE

What's the best way to smuggle gold onto a plane? Considering how heavy gold is, two Sri Lankan men will tell you it's a bad idea to try hiding it in your rectum.

According to *The Guardian*, a forty-five-year-old man was arrested in September 2017 after he was spotted "behaving suspiciously" in a Sri Lankan airport lounge. "He was called for a thorough screening after customs officers noticed him walking with difficulty and appearing to be in pain," customs spokesman Sunil Jayaratne said.

Metal detectors then identified the hidden contraband—904 grams of gold, worth about $30,000—"carefully packed in polythene bags and neatly inserted" into his rectum. Among the items recovered were seven gold "biscuits" and six chains. All of the goods were confiscated, and the man was fined.

This was not the first time that someone had attempted to conceal gold in their rectum. In 2015 *The Guardian* reported that Sri Lankan authorities had caught a man who was arguably even more ambitious when using his behind as a storage facility. In his case, the precious cargo consisted of gold bars weighing a total of 400 grams. Customs officers' suspicions were aroused because of his inability to walk normally with so much gold inside him.

Authorities believe the men were smuggling the gold to India to increase their profit margins.

WIPE OUT

British media had a field day when two doped-up thieves were caught stealing £14,000 worth of nappy cream [bum cream for babies, for the non-British]. The crime was confusing for everyone involved, especially the police, who could not determine why an eighteen-year-old culprit was working with a fifty-two-year-old convict. As the *Rotherham Advertiser* reported, the teenager was a first-time offender, while the older individual had 47 convictions for 106 offenses, 63 of which were for theft.

The two were observed stealing the cream out of the back of a delivery truck. Police were notified, and they rapidly tracked down the Ford Transit van the two had been seen driving. According to the driver of the delivery truck, the stolen cream was worth £14,000, although the judge presiding over the case was quick to point out that it was unclear whether that was the wholesale or retail value. It was also unclear what the two men were intending to do with the cream.

THE BUTT OF THE JOKE

The result of an unintended butt-dial tends to range between funny and embarrassing for most people. It rarely leads to the police knocking on your door. But that is exactly what happened to a Pennsylvania man and his friends after he butt-dialed 911.

A 911 operator was seconds away from hanging up on an obvious accidental butt-dial when his interest was piqued by the oblivious men's conversation. According to *Time* magazine, the operator overheard the men discussing selling stolen electronics in a scheme to buy cocaine.

If that wasn't lucky enough for police, the dispatcher also managed to overhear another conversation going on in the same room, in which someone was arranging to meet up with a drug dealer. The discussion included a mention of the men's current location, leading the police right to them.

Upon arrival, the police recovered both electronics and suspicious syringes. The men attempted to deny ownership, with one man even going so far as to lie about his name, allowing the police to slap him with a false identification charge. The other two men were not charged.

The only man charged pleaded guilty and was sentenced to fifteen to thirty days in jail. *Time* reported that he told the judge he was "happy" with that sentence.

A KINDER SURPRISE

"Dominic" wanted to go back to prison so badly, he threw a rock at a police car that was parked in front of a courthouse in Ottawa, Ontario. His ploy worked, especially since he was already on probation for earlier offenses. He was arrested, held for bail and transported to jail. Things were going according to plan.

Dominic, twenty at the time, was plotting to get into the Ottawa-Carleton Detention Centre because he wanted to smuggle contraband into the prison, the *Ottawa Citizen* reported. He had the plastic inner containers from eight Kinder Surprise eggs—foil-wrapped chocolate eggs whose containers usually hold small toys, but in this case were packed with drugs and related paraphernalia—in his rectum, a practice known in jails as "hooping."

Containers from the hollow centers of the popular chocolate treat—an Italian product, despite its German name (*kinder* means "children")—are one of the most popular objects for smuggling contraband into Canadian jails. Apparently, the ovoid yellow vessels are relatively easy to hoop.

Unfortunately for Dominic, a guard at the jail became suspicious when Dominic was exhibiting signs of discomfort. The guard placed him in a "dry cell," meaning that it has no plumbing, and waited for the suspected contraband to make its appearance.

Apparently, having eight Kinder containers shoved up your rectum is pretty uncomfortable, as Dominic ended up removing them himself. A guard collected and photographed them before placing them in the jail's drug safe. They contained 59 grams of marijuana, a gram of MDMA (a.k.a. ecstasy or molly), tobacco, rolling papers and matches—an extraordinary feat considering the containers really aren't *that* big.

Dominic pleaded guilty to drug trafficking in September 2017 and was sentenced to two years, with 250 days already having been served during pretrial custody.

Dominic's hooping of eight Kinder eggs is believed to be a record, easily topping a case involving four eggs in 2010.

OUT OF CIRCULATION

When a Marion County, Florida, deputy pulled over "Patrick," twenty-six, for speeding in the early hours of a Saturday in

August 2017, Patrick knew he was in trouble. He was well aware that a search of the car would reveal methamphetamine, rock cocaine and heroin, as well as a scale.

He was right, as police quickly found all that and more. Patrick was also carrying a "small amount of marijuana and a large amount of currency on his person." They arrested him and brought him to Marion County Jail.

But Patrick wasn't going down without a fight. As police reported in a Facebook post, when they arrived at the jail, the money they had found earlier was missing. Patrick claimed that deputies had already collected it, but "this was certainly not true," police said. It was then that "detention deputies . . . observed $20 bills falling from Patrick's buttocks area." In a process dubbed "necessary but undesirable" for everyone, they retrieved $1,090 hidden in Patrick's rectum.

Police also revealed that there was a seven-month-old child in the front passenger seat of Patrick's car when he was arrested. Patrick was charged with several offenses relating to the possession of marijuana and drug equipment, smuggling contraband into a detention facility and trafficking methamphetamine, heroin and cocaine. Patrick had previously been sentenced for drug-related offenses in 2013.

NEED A DIAPER CHANGE? DEPENDS

Some criminals are not just dumb, they're weird. "Ethan," a twenty-five-year-old who wants people to change his diapers, is right up there among the weirdest.

According to *HuffPost*, in March 2011, Ethan, of Hooksett, New Hampshire, posted an ad on Craigslist saying that he needed an in-home nurse to care for his son, who had a severe brain injury that he had sustained in a car accident. When a nurse responded to the ad, she found Ethan alone in the house, behaving as if he were cognitively impaired. Believing him to be incapable of taking care of himself, she changed his diaper.

But when no one contacted her to schedule further visits, she became suspicious and notified police. Ethan was arrested on a charge of indecent exposure. "He exposed himself and it caused alarm to this nurse," Hooksett Police detective Janet Bouchard said. "He brought her there under false pretenses."

Ethan was indicted in September 2012 on charges of attempted indecent exposure and lewdness. But, as *Seacoastonline.com* reported, after a plea deal in May 2013, he had his prison sentence deferred and was released on parole—as long as he behaved himself. Among other conditions of his release, it was forbidden for him to have unsupervised access to the internet.

Unfortunately, good behavior proved impossible for Ethan. On July 28, as his parole officer, Norman Marquis, later wrote in an affidavit, Ethan contacted an adult-care agency called Personal Touch Home Care (no doubt the name appealed to him), using an alias and claiming to have a disabled son who needed a diaper change.

One of the terms of Ethan's parole was that Marquis could put him in jail for one to five days if he violated a condition of his release. After the Hooksett Police Department received a report about the incident, Marquis used his authority to jail Ethan for five days, ending on August 2.

Then, on August 15, Ethan bought a prepaid phone and used it to get the contact information for an in-home childcare service in New Boston, New Hampshire. He drove there and asked a caregiver to change his soiled diaper. She refused—although she later told police she could smell the evidence that a diaper change was necessary.

In a meeting on August 20, Marquis confronted Ethan with information from a police report about his actions five days earlier, but Ethan "continuously denied" that he had been in New Boston that day. "The defendant lied to me several times," Marquis wrote in his affidavit. Ethan eventually buckled under Marquis's questioning and admitted his guilt in the New Boston incident. He confessed that he "had a conversation with the victim and admitted to bringing a duffle bag full of diapers, wipes and a box of gloves," Marquis wrote. "He states he then destroyed the phone in the Merrimack River and put the other items in his garbage."

Marquis told the court it was his "grave concern that [Ethan] is becoming an increasingly significant risk to public safety in his current condition." Prosecutors asked the judge to impose Ethan's original sentence, and he agreed, sentencing Ethan to two to four years in state prison for violating the terms of his parole.

A natural question might be whether Ethan suffered from a mental health disorder, but according to his own testimony, he hadn't been diagnosed with one. As we said, some people are just weird.

DRUG BUST

HE FAILED HIS METH TEST

"Dylan," forty-nine, of Hawthorne, Florida, had a sneaking suspicion that he had been scammed by his dealer after he had a "violent reaction" to the meth he had purchased a week earlier. Hoping to find evidence against the dealer, Dylan did what any concerned drug user would do: he called the police and asked them to check the product for him.

"The suspect said he believed because of the 'violent reaction' he had after smoking the drug, he was sold the wrong narcotic," the Putnam County Sheriff's Office said in a Facebook post in June 2018. "[Dylan] told detectives in the drug unit he wanted the substance tested because he wanted to 'press charges' on the person who sold him the wrong narcotic."

According to CNN, the detectives were happy to oblige and told Dylan to come to the sheriff's office. Dylan drove to the facility and handed investigators a foil packet containing a clear, crystal-like substance. True to their word, police tested the contents of the packet, which did, in fact, prove to be methamphetamine.

Unsurprisingly, Dylan was charged with possession and taken next door to the Putnam County Jail.

"Remember, our detectives are always ready to assist anyone who believes they were misled in their illegal drug purchase," the sheriff's office said in the post.

Similarly, in May 2018, police in Gratis, Ohio, offered in a Facebook post to test meth for the Zika virus. According to the Centers for

Disease Control and Prevention, outbreaks of the mosquito-borne disease have occurred mainly in South America, Central America and Mexico—in other words, not really all that close to Ohio. The viral infection, for which there is no vaccine and no known cure, can be transmitted during pregnancy to a fetus in the womb, causing severe birth defects. As the *Independent* reported, however, the Gratis Police Department was quite candid in its post, helpfully providing the disclaimer that meth cannot act as a host to Zika.

A REAL DOZER

A resident of Pengam, South Wales, came downstairs one morning in September 2016 and, looking outside, was startled to spot twenty-seven-year-old "Seth" asleep in a hammock in her garden.

As reported by *WalesOnline*, the woman called the police, who arrived quickly, removed a knife from Seth, woke him and asked if he knew where he was. He said he was in Llandaff, a Cardiff suburb about 15 miles away. The officers saw that Seth's pupils were dilated and his body was "jerking." They found two grams of amphetamine in his pockets.

Later, Seth told police, "I was off my head. I didn't know what I was doing."

When asked why he was carrying the knife, he replied, "God knows."

Prosecutor Stuart McLeese told Cardiff Crown Court that Seth had damaged a window and broken a padlock, and had burgled three sheds on the property, leaving items scattered around the garden. McLeese said, "He apologized to the home owner as he was removed."

The court heard that Seth had twenty-nine convictions for 112 offenses, including several burglaries, and had been released from his previous sentence just a month before dozing off in the woman's garden.

Seth pleaded guilty to shed burglary, carrying a knife in a public place and possession of amphetamine. He was sentenced to sixteen months in prison.

LIVING THE HIDE LIFE

When "Giorgio" posted photos of his luxurious life on Facebook, the fugitive Italian gangster didn't think the police would notice. But detectives in Naples did, and in March 2017, Giorgio was captured in Mexico.

According to a report from *Business Insider*, Giorgio, sixty-five, who was calling himself "Silvio Galucci," looked relaxed and happy in the photos, taken at the beach or with his arm around an attractive woman. Police said Giorgio had remarried and had children in Mexico.

At the time, he was living in the port city of Tampico, in northeastern Mexico. The city was once known as the center of Mexico's oil industry, but had more recently become the hub from which Mexico's most brutal drug cartels ran their smuggling operations.

Back in Naples, where Giorgio was born, detectives were studying Galucci's Facebook timeline, seeking to confirm his real identity. They suspected he was actually Giorgio—a convicted drug smuggler who had been running from the law for almost twenty-five years— because they had discovered that "Galucci" was Giorgio's mother's maiden name.

Their efforts were "part of a larger strategy being coordinated by the anti-crime division of the Italian police to capture mafia fugitives who have been taking refuge abroad for many years," Italian authorities said in a statement.

Giorgio and his former wife had originally been arrested in January 1993 while they were transporting 16 kilograms of cocaine to the Camorra, a criminal organization based in Naples. Giorgio was said to be a high-level member of the Camorra, and had been on Italy's Ten Most Wanted list for more than a decade. Police sources said he had collaborated with the Mazzarella, Formicola, Polverino and Tolomelli crime families, and was one of the bosses in an operation that smuggled cocaine into Germany in the 1980s and '90s.

Giorgio was officially labeled a fugitive in 1998 after a Naples court found him guilty of international drug trafficking and sentenced him to twenty-two years in jail. The sentence was passed *in absentia*, since Giorgio had disappeared in 1994 while awaiting trial.

After his new identity was confirmed in 2017, agents from the Mexican Criminal Investigation Agency and Interpol detained Giorgio near his Tampico home, then flew him directly to Rome, where Naples police met him and escorted him to jail.

CAUGHT IN THE APP

In the same week as "Giorgio's" apprehension, another Italian, facing more than five years in jail in Italy for drug trafficking, was captured in the Caribbean resort city of Playa del Carmen.

The Yucatan Times reported that "Mario," thirty-four, had been showing off on social media, posting photos of his lavish lifestyle—having fun at the beach, partying with various women, working out—using his real name, even though he was wanted by Interpol.

According to Italian police, between 2013 and 2014, Mario was involved in several drug-trafficking operations, moving more than 132 pounds of hashish between Spain and Italy. He had been sentenced to five years and seven months in prison.

In May 2016, Mario was categorized as a fugitive. In October, Interpol issued a warrant for his arrest, but he had already fled the country. Police said he first went to Spain, then moved on to Mexico, entering on a tourist visa but staying on illegally in the Yucatan beach town, where he set up a restaurant and managed a gym.

The fact that he used his real name online helped Mexican and Italian authorities in their collaborative efforts to track Mario down. He was picked up by officers from the Mexican Attorney General's Office and delivered straight to Italian authorities.

SWEET JUSTICE

A woman in Springfield, Missouri, was understandably furious when she found out the "cocaine" she had purchased from a local dealer was actually just sugar. So she did what any rational person would do: she called the police to complain. According to the *Daily Mail*, the woman demanded that police secure a full refund for her. As one would expect, police promptly charged her for possession of drug paraphernalia after finding a crack pipe on her.

THE SUSPECT WAS A GAS

When police interviewed "Stan," twenty-five, in September 2017 about drugs and handguns found in a car in which he was a passenger, he was reasonably cooperative, answering every question, although he denied any knowledge of the illegal items. However, the officers still found him to be insufferable. Why? His answers were punctuated by farts.

After a detective asked the Kansas City man for his address, for example, Stan "leaned to one side of his chair and released a loud fart before answering with the address," according to the police record of the interrogation. The detective added, "[Stan] continued to be flatulent and I ended the interview."

No charges were filed at the time. However, Stan was arrested a couple of months later on federal gun and drug charges. This time, police had found marijuana and crack cocaine inside a vehicle he was driving, as well as a .38-caliber revolver that had been reported stolen.

In October 2018, he pleaded guilty in U.S. District Court to one count of possession with intent to sell cocaine, heroin and marijuana, and using a firearm in furtherance of a drug crime.

APPARENTLY, TREES ARE FLAMMABLE

Addict "Sherri" was sheltering in a hollow spot in the root system of the Senator, the world's largest and oldest bald cypress tree, when she decided she needed some light to see the drugs she wanted to take. So she set a fire inside the tree. This wasn't her best idea, but you could probably call it her brightest.

As reported by *The New York Times*, the fire quickly burned out of control, destroying the giant tree, which was 125 feet tall, 18 feet wide and about 3,500 years old. Located in Seminole County, Florida, it was the biggest tree east of the Mississippi, and the fifth-largest in the United States.

The fire was first seen at the top of the tree, which had burned from the inside out, "like a chimney." Firefighters tried to extinguish the blaze, but the tree collapsed. Its charred remains now stand only 20 to 25 feet tall.

At first, the tree was thought to have been destroyed by a lightning strike. Sherri's role was discovered later, in part because officials found images on her laptop and her cell phone that showed the twenty-six-year-old model starting the fire.

The incident happened in Big Tree Park, near Longwood, Florida, in January 2012. Court records and the arrest report show that Sherri had hopped over a fence and was inside a hollow part of the base of the tree when she set fire to some debris so she could see her drugs.

The *Daily Mail* wrote that Circuit Judge John Galluzzo gave Sherri a thirty-month suspended prison sentence, saying that if she could successfully complete five years of probation, she could remain free. But that didn't happen.

In October 2015, a police officer in Casselberry, Florida, saw Sherri on a motor scooter and pulled her over. The scooter had an improper tag and wasn't registered. Sherri was given citations for the offenses, which prompted her probation officer to ask for her arrest. She was jailed in December.

In March 2016, Sherri admitted that she had violated the terms of her probation, which prohibited her from breaking the law. Circuit

Judge Donna McIntosh lifted the suspension, ended her probation and ordered Sherri to prison for thirty months, according to defense attorney Daniel Megaro. She got credit for the nearly ten months she had already served.

The Seminoles and other Native Americans in central Florida had used the tree as a landmark for hundreds, if not thousands, of years. In the late nineteenth century, the tree attracted visitors even though the surrounding land was mostly swamp. People reached the tree by jumping from log to log. A walkway was constructed by the Works Progress Administration in the 1930s.

In 1925, a hurricane destroyed the top of the tree, reducing its height from 165 feet to 118 feet.

The Senator was named for Florida State Senator Moses Overstreet, who donated the tree and surrounding land to Seminole County for a park in 1927.

In March 2014, Big Tree Park was reopened to the public after being closed for almost a year. Some people believe the tree is still alive, as saplings have been seen at its base, and it is said that a Senator clone has been located and is growing at the entrance to the park, near the playground.

Just 40 feet from the Senator's remains is another old cypress, named Lady Liberty, which was considered the Senator's companion tree. It is 89 feet high and 10 feet in diameter, and is estimated to be 2,000 years old.

YOU'RE HISTORY!

TROJAN TRUNK

Here is a rags-to-riches story like no other.

Barbara Erni was born into poverty in 1743 in Feldkirch, Austria, but she managed to rise above her circumstances with the use of a large trunk that she carried around Europe throughout the latter half of the eighteenth century. According to *Atlas Obscura*, Erni, said to be a strong, beautiful woman, told everyone the trunk contained her collection of precious items. However, what it actually contained was a small man (or, as some reports stated, a large child).

This was her con: Erni would check into an inn and tell the innkeeper that the trunk had to be locked into the most secure room in the building. The innkeeper would comply, placing it in the room where all the valuables belonging to the inn and the guests were kept. Then, when everyone was asleep, the person in the trunk would let himself out, load the trunk with the room's most portable and valuable items, and escape into the night with Erni.

Liechtensteinian legend says Erni would tramp through Europe from inn to inn, stealing valuables and whatever other items her accomplice could find. Unfortunately, her partner's identity has been lost to history.

It was a simple scheme, and thanks in part to the time in which she was working, Erni managed to keep it going for nearly fifteen years. She accrued great wealth during those years.

In May 1784, Liechtensteinian authorities finally apprehended Erni and her tiny accomplice in the town of Eschen and put them on trial. Erni pleaded guilty to seventeen separate burglaries, and she and her partner were sentenced to death by beheading. Her sentence was carried out on February 26, 1785, before a public audience of 1,000. The fate of her male assistant is unknown.

KEEP YOUR POWDER DRY

You might remember from history class the Gunpowder Plot of 1605, but in case you don't, it was an attempt by a group of Catholics to assassinate King James I of England, who was a Protestant.

The group's plot involved planting a gunpowder bomb near the king and blowing him up. Unfortunately for them, before they could light the fuse, the head bomber, Guy Fawkes, was captured and his explosives confiscated.

Committed to their cause, some of Fawkes's co-conspirators eluded capture and decided to carry on with their plan. However, their remaining gunpowder was damp and wouldn't detonate. The revolutionaries decided they needed to dry it. And how do you dry things? With heat. Where do you get heat? Fire.

According to the BBC, the rebels built a fire to dry the wet gunpowder. Predictably, it exploded, in the process blinding the Catholic rebellion's new leader, John Grant.

So they decided to just attack Warwick Castle head-on, and were defeated immediately. Every rebel was either captured or killed, and often both.

You might say the revolution bombed.

DUEL CITIZENS

Perth, Ontario, which is located halfway between Ottawa and Kingston, was the backdrop for one of Canada's most tragic love stories, a clash between friends that would wind up being the last fatal duel to take place in Canada.

As the *Ottawa Citizen* describes, it was a rainy morning on June 13, 1833, when Robert Lyon, age twenty, fell after being shot by twenty-three-year-old John Wilson. Wilson and Lyon were law students who had both come to Perth to study under prominent lawyers. Both had been born in Scotland, but each of their families had decided to move to Canada when the boys were young. Despite this similarity, their families belonged to vastly different classes. While Lyon's was aristocratic, Wilson's was far humbler, and Wilson had to support himself during his studies.

In Perth, Wilson met and became friends with Lyon, and the two of them met Elizabeth Hughes, a young schoolteacher from England. Wilson was quite taken by Miss Hughes, but she did not reciprocate his affections. Disappointed, Wilson left for Ottawa.

While he was gone, another suitor, Henri LeLievre, arrived in Perth. LeLievre was a friend of Lyon's, and the two young men took Hughes on a date together, during which it was said that Lyon put "his arms about her in a position which no woman of spirit would permit," according to one account in the *Ottawa Citizen*.

Wilson, upon hearing the news, was furious. Even though Lyon said the whole thing was a joke meant to make Wilson jealous, the two soon met on the streets of Perth and got into a fight. Lyon won the fight handily, and Wilson, badly beaten, asked if they could work things out. Lyon refused, so Wilson challenged Lyon to a duel, and this time Lyon accepted.

The pistol duel took place on the outskirts of town. Wilson had, as his second, a man named Simon Robertson, and Lyon was assisted by his friend LeLievre. According to the surgeon at the scene, both men missed their first shots. Wilson and Lyon suggested that they could reconcile, but LeLievre urged them to continue, saying that honor demanded a clear resolution. So they fired again. This time, Wilson's bullet pierced Lyon's right breast, killing him. Feeling terrible about killing his friend, Wilson turned himself in to the local authorities.

Wilson and Robertson were both charged with murder, though they were eventually acquitted. Wilson acted as his own lawyer, presenting a passionate self-defense. After leaving Perth in 1834 to open a law practice in London, Ontario, he married Elizabeth Hughes, whose attitude seems to have changed after the duel.

LeLievre fled the country immediately after the incident and is believed to have died in Australia.

Today, Robert Lyon's grave rests in a small cemetery outside of Perth, allegedly just a few yards away from where he died. His plain headstone, worn after so many years, reads: "Friendship Offering Dedicated to the Memory of ROBERT LYON, Student at law. He fell in mortal combat, 13 of June 1833 in the 20th year of his Age, Requiescat in Pace."

Today, the pistols from this final duel reside in the Perth Museum, and the site of the event itself is now immortalized as Last Duel Park.

BLIND AMBITION

"Russell" committed countless bank heists and attempted eleven jailbreaks. That's especially impressive considering that, at the time of an article published by *People* magazine in 1990, he had spent twenty-five years behind bars and had been legally blind for most of his life. In fact, Russell blamed his blindness for his life of crime. "My eyes got so bad I had to turn to robbery," he said. As *People* put it, "the forty-two-year-old bank robber's hindsight has always been 20-20. It's his eyesight that has failed him."

Suffering from the incurable degenerative eye disease retinitis pigmentosa, Russell became completely blind in the 1980s while a resident of Lompoc Federal Penitentiary, a maximum-security prison north of Santa Barbara, California.

Born in San Pedro, California, Russell started his first scam at sixteen. He would collect a $5 "application fee" from people eager to work from home, specifically stuffing envelopes. But no envelope-stuffing work ever arrived.

Russell was convicted of mail fraud in 1973 and did some time in the federal prison in Springfield, Missouri, where he heard that federally insured banks instruct tellers not to resist during robberies—to simply turn the cash over. Russell pulled off his first heist in March 1974, immediately after being released from prison.

"I told the cab driver I had to go by the bank to pick up some money," Russell said. And pick it up he did: while the cab waited, the teller put $8,000 into a brown paper bag and Russell unfolded his white cane and tapped his way out the door.

His next job was in 1977, *People* recounted. "The bank guard opened the door for me and thanked me as I left," Russell said.

It took him "seven or eight" jobs to perfect his technique. He would focus his slightly less bad right eye on the back of someone's shoe, then follow that person to the teller's window. "Young people walk too fast, so I'd wait for older people."

When he got to the window, he'd give the teller his calling card, a one-eyed jack on which was written, "Be quick, be quiet, or you're dead. Put all the cash in the bag. I have a gun." (He usually didn't, and if he did, it was an unloaded pellet gun.) Then he would beat a careful retreat to the door.

But in September 1977, as he was feeling his way out of a Citibank branch in New York City, he stumbled into armed guards who were delivering money, and he was arrested.

Russell spent the next six years in jail in New York. After his release in February 1983, the halfway house to which he had been assigned refused to accept him because he was blind, and he was put back on the street.

Shortly thereafter, Russell walked into the nearest Citibank, which he says was known in the criminal world for its shortage of guards. Holding a soft-drink bottle under his prison-issued coat to mimic a gun, Russell walked off with $18,000, his biggest haul yet.

Russell flew to Las Vegas and spent the money on showgirls. He also made a list of all the Citibank branches in New York, using a small scope to read the Manhattan phone book.

For three months, Russell commuted between Las Vegas and New York. He'd fly into New York, take a cab to the bank, rob it, take the cab back to the airport and return to Las Vegas. He estimates that, during this time, he managed to deposit $71,000 in a Las Vegas bank under an assumed name.

Russell's downfall came when he varied his routine, visiting a discount store after a heist. This detour gave police enough time to send out officers, who spotted him on the street. Russell was charged with nine counts of armed bank robbery and sentenced to seventeen years in jail. He attempted to escape from jail eleven times, one time making it over two hurricane fences before getting caught.

Russell did claim to have given a lot of what he stole to charity, including $35,000 to retinitis pigmentosa research.

The National Federation of the Blind has said that the urge to commit crimes isn't limited to the sighted. "We have about as much virtue and as much vice as everybody else, and some of us are inclined to abide by the law while others remain unabashedly outside the legal system."

FLY AWAY HOME

A man who attempted to blackmail the Swiss company Nestlé by injecting cyanide into its products was finally captured after his homing-pigeon scheme went awry.

"Andrei," forty-three, admitted that he had demanded 25 million deutsche marks' worth of diamonds, which he had planned to be placed in small pouches hung around the necks of pigeons trained to find their way home to him.

As reported by The Independent, Andrei had poisoned several Nestlé products in more than twenty cities across Germany over a period of two years. He would allegedly travel from city to city, leaving cyanide-laced drinks and sauces in playgrounds and supermarkets. The police eventually captured him when a pigeon named Charly led them to Andrei's location, where he had been hiding out and training his birds.

Andrei said he thought he had planned a foolproof scheme, but had since realized his mistake: the pigeons were inevitably following an easily trackable flight path straight back to his home.

As a result, police had no trouble catching him. All they had to do was place a tiny signal beacon on the birds, instead of a pouch of diamonds, and follow the avian accomplices in a helicopter to where the blackmailer was waiting.

In September 1999, a Frankfurt regional court found Andrei guilty of three counts of extortion and six counts of poisoning food products. He was sentenced to eleven years in jail.

Andrei told the court he realized he had played a dangerous game by poisoning mustard, mayonnaise and other foodstuffs, and he was glad no one had died.

"It was extremely lucky that that did not happen," he admitted after being sentenced, "but I was convinced that the strong smell would put anyone off from eating."

I DID IT ALL FOR LOVE (OR MAYBE SEX)

HE SAID IT WAS BIGAMY

"Spencer," fifty-four, invited eighty people to help celebrate his second marriage in October 2017, even though he was still married to his first wife. Here is a pro tip for all those planning illegal weddings: don't invite eighty people. And definitely don't invite eighty people if most of them are still friends with your first wife.

The wedding between Spencer and "Andrea" took place in Pemberton, England. According to *Wigan Today*, Spencer's first wife, "Sadie" said she was "absolutely shocked and quite upset" after she found out her estranged husband had wed another woman. The couple had separated in 2010 after sixteen years together, but there had been no discussions about making the separation official. Not until Sadie found out about the surprise wedding from her friends and family, that is.

Appearing at Wigan and Leigh Magistrates' Court in March 2019, Spencer pleaded guilty to bigamy and was given a twelve-month community sentence and ordered to complete 100 hours of volunteer work and to pay £170 in costs.

As reported by *Wigan Today*, lawyer Tess Kenyon, speaking on behalf of Sadie, told the court, "[My client] says it was when Spencer received information from [Sadie's] solicitor about a financial settlement that he realized there was a problem with the divorce and he shouldn't have gone ahead with the marriage."

Spencer and Sadie attended Wigan Family Court in December 2017, two months after Spencer's marriage to Andrea. Sadie claimed that she had questioned her ex about the marriage because she had seen a video of the event, and he had lied, telling her that the October event was just a ceremony and not a marriage.

Kenyon told the magistrates' court, "She accepted this account because he was clearly still married to her at that point."

However, Sadie became suspicious, so she contacted the vicar of the Pemberton church and was told the wedding had been official.

Nick Lloyd, defending Spencer, said divorce proceedings had started before any plans were made for the wedding, and his client was unaware that there had been a delay in granting the divorce decrees.

Andrea, who attended court with Spencer, said she was standing by her would-be husband, and they hoped to have a smaller but legal wedding later in the year.

A REAL JOHNNY-COME-LATELY

"Alexis," a forty-seven-year-old prison guard at HMP Garth, in Lancashire, England, was infatuated with gangster inmate Marcus. So she did what any infatuated prison guard would do: she attempted to smuggle out a syringe containing his sperm.

Alexis was caught when the syringe was found in her purse during a routine search. After this discovery, the police searched her home. In her underwear drawer, they found a letter from the inmate.

Alexis was given a nine-month sentence after being convicted of misconduct in a public office. The *Mirror* reported that, during her trial, the jury was told Alexis was "besotted" with Marcus and had recently told a friend she wanted to have a baby with him.

Marcus was weeks away from parole when their affair was

discovered in October 2014. Marcus and his brother had been imprisoned in 2007 for commanding a brutal gang that hijacked cars and kidnapped motorists around Greater Manchester.

Alexis's friend told Preston Crown Court that Alexis had collected the semen after Marcus slipped it under his cell door. According to the *Mirror*, Alexis had told her friend that she planned to use the syringe "like a turkey baster" to get pregnant.

In his sentencing, Judge Simon Newell said, "Inappropriate relationships between staff and prisoners are very dangerous and can often lead to other criminal activity. . . . Those who choose to cross the line and form inappropriate relationships put the general public, including staff and visitors to the prison, at very significant risk."

The court heard a number of testimonials advocating for Alexis, describing her as a kind-hearted woman. But Newell said there must be zero tolerance for inappropriate prison relationships and declared that he must hand down a deterrent sentence.

Marcus was not charged with anything in regard to his relationship with Alexis.

BUS-TED

Passengers on a National Express coach traveling through Devon, England, got quite the show when a man and a woman reportedly stripped off and had sex right there on the bus.

According to a report by *BirminghamLive*, it happened just after 10 p.m. on a Monday in March 2019. The two people had met for the first time on the ten-hour-long trip from Manchester to Exeter.

Devon and Cornwall Police arrested the pair and took them into police custody after the driver brought the bus to a sudden halt on the shoulder of the M5 highway.

A police spokesperson said, "Police were called to an incident of public indecency on a coach traveling on the M5 near Cullompton. . . . Officers located and arrested a twenty-nine-year-old man from Bristol and a thirty-two-year-old woman from Barnstaple on suspicion of an act of outraging public decency. They were later released under investigation pending further enquiries."

A spokesperson for National Express said, "We are aware of an alleged incident on board a vehicle travelling between Blackpool and Plymouth . . . and will assist the police with any investigation."

In a similar incident in Toronto, Ontario, in 2011, a couple openly had sex while on a subway car. They were booted from the train and continued their amorous adventure on the platform, in full view of passengers. When police arrived, the couple was charged with lewd behavior. In 2014, another couple was nabbed by investigators for participating in a "sexual activity incident" on a streetcar.

THERE'S A FIRST TIME FOR EVERYTHING

A Brazilian woman who auctioned off her virginity for $780,000 says she was defrauded by filmmaker "Jensen," who organized the auction and told her that he would be making a documentary, titled *Virgins Wanted*, that would feature the event.

Twenty-year-old "Cristina" made headlines in 2012 when she announced the auction. But *HuffPost* reported that when Cristina met the successful bidder—a Japanese millionaire known only as

Noritaka—in 2013, the meeting did not go well. He didn't look like the person who had been described to her, she said, nor did he cover her travel expenses as promised. She returned to Brazil *virgo intacta* and claimed that she never received any money.

To those wondering about the legal issues surrounding selling your virginity (otherwise known as prostitution), Jensen explained that the event would occur in a plane over international waters.

Jensen's attempts to make the documentary had been in the news since 2010. After realizing the public interest, Jensen announced that he was going to create a reality TV show based on the same premise. He reported that he was receiving messages from hundreds of people who wanted to auction their virginity.

Cristina argues that Jensen was using the documentary as a way to defraud people, and that he still owes her some of the money he was earning from the documentary by selling it worldwide as a reality TV show. She says she was supposed to get 20 percent of the documentary sales and all of the money from the auction, but she got neither.

According to *HuffPost*, Jensen has denied all of Cristina's allegations and alleges that she breached their contract on at least two occasions. Nor does he believe Cristina is still a virgin. "We have the footage to prove otherwise," he said.

While some people think having sex for money is the basic definition of prostitution, Cristina disagrees. "If you only do it once in your life, then you are not a prostitute," she said, "just like if you take one amazing photograph it does not automatically make you a photographer. The auction is just business, I'm a romantic girl at heart and I believe in love."

A second auction Cristina tried to conduct herself in late 2013 was also unsuccessful, although she claims to have received a bid of $440,000.

In early 2014, Cristina proposed a Brazilian reality show in which twenty men would compete for a $1 million prize—and her virginity. However, nothing came of it.

WELL GROOMED

Wedding-day traditions are a wonderful thing: something old, something new, throwing the bouquet and the garter, clinking glasses to get the happy couple to kiss, beating up the groom and chasing him into traffic to get hit by a car . . . wait, what?

According to *The Telegraph*, wedding guests in China traditionally play pranks on the bride and groom in a ritual of "wedding hazing" that dates back to the days of arranged marriages. The light-hearted pranks were originally intended to break the ice between the newlyweds and to ward off evil spirits.

Unfortunately for "Chanming," his friends really didn't seem to understand the spirit of the tradition. On his wedding day in November 2018, they took things way too far. When Chanming was on his way to pick up his wife-to-be, they intercepted him, threw eggs, beer and ink on him, stripped him down to his skivvies, bound him to an electric pole and used a bamboo stick to beat him. This was all well and good, apparently, but for Chanming, throwing ink in his face was a step too far.

"Someone was chasing me and I couldn't see very well because of the ink, then somehow I ran onto a motorway with someone tailing me behind," he told a local website.

A BMW swerved in an attempt to avoid Chanming but crashed into and ricocheted off the road barricade, hitting him anyway and knocking him down.

Chanming suffered internal bleeding and a skull fracture, and was hospitalized for three weeks. But it gets worse: the police held him responsible for the accident, and the driver's insurance company presented him with a bill for $4,372 in damages to the car.

After all this, Tribune Media Wire reported, Chanming was planning on suing his friends to help cover the bill.

AUTOMATIC FAILURES

STICKING IT TO THEM

Even after trying a second time, two teens in Nashville, Tennessee, could not figure out how to successfully complete a carjacking. According to a Nashville Police Department press release, officers arrested two "young men," ages fifteen and seventeen, in August 2018 after they attempted to carjack two women in separate incidents. "Attempted" being the key word, as neither carjacking was successful.

In their first attempt, the release said, a woman was in her vehicle in a parking garage. The teens ran up to the car, one on each side, and "yelled for her to get out" before trying to yank her out of the car. The woman stood her ground, pressing down on the horn and scaring them into running off.

Wanting a chance at redemption after their first failure, the duo tried again an hour later, at around 7:30 p.m. A woman had just parked her car at a Kroger supermarket and was walking toward the store when one of them grabbed the keys out of her hand. They ran and climbed into her car. "After a few seconds, they exited the car and fled on foot, apparently unable to drive a manual transmission," the press release said.

The teen suspects were spotted and arrested in Nashville later that evening. After being positively identified by the victims, they were charged in juvenile court with attempted robbery and carjacking, theft of property and attempted theft of a vehicle.

IN THE CLUTCH

Four car thieves in Alabama proved once again that a manual transmission is one of the best car-theft deterrents around.

As reported by *Fox10*, four men attempted to steal a Honda Civic in the parking lot of a Quick Stop on January 28, 2019. When the men pulled up to the convenience store in Semmes, Alabama, in a black SUV, they spotted an unattended car, with the keys in the ignition, parked nearby (which is dumb in its own right, but there you go).

Two men from the SUV got into the Honda. They wanted a fast getaway, but were mystified by the stick shift and clutch pedal. They sat in the car, not moving, for so long that the owner came back and discovered them in mid-theft. When he challenged them, they gave up and ran off behind the store. The car's owner used his phone to record the SUV's driver and license plate number.

The driver was later identified by Mobile County Sheriff's Office as the man who had attempted to rob another convenience store earlier the same day, using a fake, homemade weapon. The clerk didn't take him seriously, so he settled for buying (with his own money) a six-pack of beer instead. Thank goodness he remembered to bring his wallet!

MANUAL LABOR

As soon as "Desmond" parked near his house in St. Louis, Missouri, one night in October 2016, he noticed a suspicious car behind him.

"A car came up right behind, sort of half-parallel parked behind me," Desmond told a reporter from *KMOV News*. "A passenger got out with a firearm, told me to get out of my car and empty my pockets."

Desmond took out the keys to his Nissan Altima and asked, "What do I do now?"

"Get up and walk away," the thief said. "Face away and keep walking."

Desmond complied, but his car was not stolen. He thinks the gunman, who police said was in his late teens or early twenties, didn't take the car because he couldn't drive a stick shift.

TAXI!

A Utah man who absentmindedly left the keys in his car in June 2015 thought it was a joke when he first discovered that the vehicle was gone. As reported by *AJC*, the owner was in such disbelief that he started to make his way to his brother's house, assuming the missing car was a prank. But no, the car had actually been stolen.

However, as it turns out, the nineteen-year-old guy who nicked it didn't know how to drive a stick shift, and the owner, upon locating his car a short distance away, was horrified by the sight of it lurching away, stalling and grinding gears. According to *KSL.com*, the carjacker's girlfriend knew how to drive a manual transmission, but rather than take the driver's seat, she had decided this was the perfect opportunity to teach her beau how to do it.

The would-be thieves eventually abandoned the car and called a cab from a nearby convenience store. The Cache County Sheriff's Department, already alerted by the car's owner, found the pair waiting for their taxi to arrive.

They attempted to escape on foot, but it wouldn't have mattered if they had gotten away, because the male thief had given his personal information to the cab company.

THREE TEENS, FIVE SPEED, ZERO CLUE

To be a carjacker, you must be ruthless. Ruthless enough to force an elderly woman out of her car. But it's also a good idea to know how to drive the cars you attempt to steal.

In June 2014, a seventy-year-old Seattle woman was forced from her Kia by three teenage thieves, only to get it back after they realized that none of them could drive stick. Unable to get the car moving, they fled on foot.

The car's owner discussed the attempted carjacking with CBS affiliate KIRO: "I got a five-speed in there. They couldn't figure out how to get it going."

She explained that she had gotten out of the car to get something from the trunk and was startled to hear a voice demanding her keys. She assumed it was a joke—until she looked up and saw a teenager in a hooded sweatshirt pointing a gun at her. "It's not every day you get a gun stuck in your face," the septuagenarian said.

Terrified, she dropped her keys, then stood there and watched as the teens tried to get the car going. When they finally gave up and sprinted away, she called 911 in tears.

But she's able to laugh about it now. "It was quite an interesting day," the woman told KIRO. "Let's put it that way."

GIVING HIM THE GEARS

Three men in Colorado Springs, Colorado, aggressively attempted to steal a car, even going as far as to punch the owner, before they realized that they were unable to drive the vehicle.

According to *CBS Denver*, a man had just pulled up to his house and hadn't yet gotten out of the car when three bandana-masked bandits dragged him out from behind the wheel. As he ran to his front door to tell his parents what was happening, one of the men pursued him and sucker-punched him.

Undeterred, he chased the suspect back to his car and realized that his stick shift was proving to be a challenge for the would-be getaway driver. "He is trying to put it in gear, but he's not pressing the clutch enough. So he's grinding my gears and he's pressing the gas and the E brake's up. So he's not going nowhere."

The car owner, who had minor injuries from the scuffle, suspected none of the three could drive a manual transmission. He demanded that they get out of his car, and since they couldn't make it go, they listened. But they made sure to steal his phone and a bag of tools before they left.

Police later caught one of the failed carjackers, and the man got his phone back.

SHIFT WORK

Seattle detectives believe a manual transmission is the only thing that stood between an armed thief and the car he wanted to steal in May 2015.

According to a post by the Seattle Police Department, a woman called 911 from a Wendy's restaurant around 9:30 p.m., telling police that a man had put a gun to her head and pulled her out of her 1998 Ford Mustang.

The suspect, in his late teens or early twenties and dressed in a black hooded sweatshirt, reportedly approached the woman as she sat in her car in the restaurant's parking lot. At first he just asked for directions, but things took a turn when he opened the door and told her to get out. She refused, even when he pointed the gun at her, so he decided to use force. After being thrown to the ground, the woman ran inside the restaurant and called the police.

When the responding officers arrived on the scene, however, they found the car still in the parking lot. Once again, a manual transmission came through in the clutch.

IN THE FIRST PLACE

Another would-be carjacker was foiled when he tried to steal a car with a stick shift in San Diego, California. Two teenagers were sitting in the car around 10:45 p.m. in February 2018, when a young man approached the passenger window and demanded their phones, *Fox 5* reported. He then ordered the eighteen- and seventeen-year-old victims to get out of the car.

"They got out and the suspect got in and tried to drive away," police officer Robert Heims said. "He revved the engine several times but the car did not go. It appeared the suspect did not know how to drive a manual and got out and ran away."

TRANSMISSION

According to the *Los Angeles Times*, a wannabe car thief was sitting inside a vehicle a little after midnight one Sunday in February 2015. The car's owner didn't realize he was there and got into the car. The thief flashed his gun and ordered the victim to drive to a nearby location. When they arrived, the thief robbed the victim and attempted to steal the car. But there was a problem: the thief couldn't work a stick shift and had to abandon the vehicle. He ended up fleeing on foot.

THE HOME STRETCH

HE CLEANED UP

In October 2014, Lancashire couple Martin Holtby and Pat Dyson returned home from their holiday feeling relaxed and refreshed. Unfortunately, this feeling quickly vanished when they discovered a burglar asleep in their bed.

According to a report in *The Telegraph*, not only had the intruder used their bed, he had made several meals, washed his dishes, cleaned the house, gone shopping for food and used the washing machine to launder his socks and underwear.

The twenty-eight-year-old Polish immigrant was given a two-year conditional discharge at Burnley Crown Court after admitting to the burglary, and was ordered to pay costs of £200.

Dyson said their house "wasn't too tidy" when they went on holiday, but the uninvited house sitter, who now lives in Leeds, had tidied up. They first realized something was wrong when they saw that their mail and newspapers had been taken inside.

Holtby said they were not threatened by their unwelcome guest. "I wasn't frightened, more surprised."

He called the police, and the man was still asleep when they arrived to arrest him.

Dyson said she felt "fairly sympathetic, although he did break in . . . but it was neatly done."

WHATSAPP?!

"Archie" of Rotherham, England, used a stolen SIM card to snap a photo of himself inside a house he was burgling. This might already seem like a bad idea on his part, but it gets worse. In an attempt to post the picture on WhatsApp, Archie also mistakenly sent the picture to the victim's work colleagues.

Unsurprisingly, the victim's colleagues reported receiving the picture to police, who tracked Archie to his home the next day, where they found a stolen Rolex watch worth £4,000 hidden behind a radiator, reported the BBC.

A spokeswoman for South Yorkshire Police said Archie and his accomplice broke into the Rotherham property in September 2013, while the occupants were on holiday. They stole electrical items, jewelry and an automobile for a total haul of about £27,000. And that SIM card, of course.

Archie, twenty-five, was jailed for two years and eight months after he admitted burglary at Sheffield Crown Court. He also admitted being in breach of a suspended sentence. His twenty-seven-year-old accomplice, also of Rotherham, was jailed for eighteen months after he admitted the offense.

But the story was not over. According to the BBC, in December 2014, Archie was sentenced to another four years for threatening to kill the victim of his earlier burglary. Archie had arranged for a menacing letter to be sent to the victim after he was jailed in March. A jury in Sheffield Crown Court found him guilty of threatening death, witness intimidation and attempting to pervert the course of justice.

A police spokesman said, "Following the original conviction for burglary, the victim in this case felt that justice had been done. Unfortunately, this was not the end of the ordeal.

"The safety and wellbeing of any victim of crime is our main priority and this sentence reflects the seriousness of threats, intimidation and attempts by anyone to pervert the course of justice."

Yeah, somebody definitely should have told Archie to quit while he was ahead.

HIT THE SHUWER

When Peter Fields came home one day in October 2016, he knew right away that something was wrong. His front door and a living room window were broken, the alarm had been torn off the wall ... and there was someone in the shower.

Fields, a contractor in Trenton, New Jersey, told *ABC13* that the brazen thief had also obviously been going through Fields's clothing—some of his clothes were packed up and arranged on his bed—and drinking his Crown Royal Canadian whisky.

"I saw him," Fields said. "I watched him. I gave the police the information while I was on the phone watching him, making sure he didn't escape. You would have thought he lived here."

Police got to the scene quickly and arrested the twenty-eight-year-old intruder while he was still soaping up.

He was charged with burglary, theft and criminal mischief, and in January 2017, he pleaded guilty to unlicensed entry of a residence, as well as to assaulting his girlfriend the previous November and using counterfeit money to buy pizza in August.

NICE GUYS FINISH LAST

It's important to be able to admit one's mistakes. Burglar "Gavin" is a big believer in this moral imperative, considering that he attempted to return a laptop he had stolen after realizing that he had robbed the wrong house. According to *The Telegraph*, Gavin had intended to break into the home and steal the belongings of someone who owed him £400. Unfortunately for Gavin, he had the wrong address, and ended up stealing the laptop of a university student. Upon realizing his mistake, Gavin was quick to try to right his wrong. He attempted to break back into the house to return the laptop, but was caught in the act and ended up being arrested.

HEADSHOT

A Kelowna, British Columbia, man attempted a home invasion and shot himself in the face instead.

"Warren," forty-nine, was arrested at Kelowna General Hospital in February 2016. One of his eyes was missing, and he had a bullet lodged in his brain. During a joint submission in Kelowna in September 2017, B.C. Supreme Court Justice Emily Burke heard that on February 17, 2016, a woman had knocked on the door of a unit at the Yaletown condominiums in Glenmore, British Columbia. When the resident opened the door, Warren and another man forced their way inside. One of the men carried a sawed-off .22-caliber rifle, and the other had a knife. During the ensuing struggle, the rifle discharged.

"We need to go. I shot myself in the face," Warren said.

He went immediately to the hospital, where he was later arrested.

According to a report from *Global News*, Warren's criminal record includes charges and convictions for theft, possession of stolen property, assaulting a peace officer, drug possession, trafficking and numerous breaches of probation and conditions.

One of two female accomplices who was with the men that night was sentenced to time served (411 days) after pleading guilty to assault.

The man with the knife, who was sentenced to three years in jail, was a young offender whose name cannot be published.

"[Warren] lost his right eye and continues to have a bullet in his brain," Justice Burke said. In sentencing him to five years for the armed robbery attempt and an additional six months for possessing a prohibited weapon, she noted that she was giving Warren the mandatory minimum sentence because he had sought treatment for the heroin addiction that drove the robbery attempt.

SAY CHEESE!

"Donovan" was handed a jail sentence of four years in 2018 after the tables were turned on him during a burglary in Folkestone, England.

As reported by *KentOnline*, the victim, upon arriving home from work, caught Donovan robbing his house. He confronted Donovan, Donovan tried to push past him, and the two men fought. Before the thief could make his getaway, the victim overpowered him, restraining him and hauling him down the stairs.

Donovan apologized and begged to be released. Eventually, the victim agreed to let him go, on one condition: he wanted to take the thief's picture. Donovan agreed, posed for the photo and left. The victim passed the photograph on to the police, who soon arrested Donovan.

Donovan received his four-year sentence after pleading guilty to burglary.

Investigating officer Richard Glass, of Kent Police, said, "While [Donovan] was previously unknown to us, we have since established he has a lengthy criminal record for other offenses of burglary and theft committed outside of Kent.

"He pleaded to be let go when caught red-handed by the victim in this case, who understandably did not want Donovan inside his home any longer than necessary.

"Instead he had the foresight to take a photograph of him, which led to Donovan's arrest."

HELP ME! I'M TRESPASSING!

In March 2011, a man called 911, asking for police to come and protect him from the owner of the home he had broken into.

According to an *ABC News* report, "Travis," twenty-four, was taking a shower in the Portland, Oregon, home when the homeowner and her daughter returned. Travis locked himself in the first-floor bathroom and called 911.

"I just broke into a house and the owners came home," he told the 911 operator. "I think they have guns." He said he wasn't sure where he was, except: "I'm up in the hills."

The owner of the house asked Travis, "Why are you in my house taking a shower?"

"I broke in," Travis said. "I was kidnapped."

He told her his name, and when she informed him that she was calling the police, he replied, "I've already called them. They're on the phone right now."

The woman called anyway, but was laughing about the whole situation as she spoke to the 911 operator. She said that she and her daughter had returned home from the grocery store, and it was her daughter who first thought there might be an intruder in the house. "My daughter said, 'You know, I hear a man in the house.' I thought, oh no, don't be silly." She also told the operator that Travis was "obviously nuts."

Travis told police that he had been kidnapped by a group of men and forced into the bathroom.

Sergeant Pete Simpson of the Portland Police Department said, "Based on what I learned last night, maybe there's some issues with mental health or substance abuse or both."

Although he did not steal anything, Travis was charged with criminal trespassing. Simpson said, "It appeared more as though he wasn't intent to steal . . . he just wanted to take a shower."

THE FRAUDS
ARE AGAINST YOU

OFFSIDE

A con man who stole significant amounts of money from one of England's Premier League soccer stars and the team's former manager was sentenced in January 2017.

The *Manchester Evening News* reported that "Jeremy," posing as Manchester City's Spanish soccer star David Silva, was able to withdraw more than £20,000 from cash machines. He then plundered £100,000 from the bank account of the team's former manager, Manuel Pellegrini, and tried to pay for a £27,000 watch with a bank card he had obtained in Pellegrini's name. Upon discovering that the card had been canceled and his name was being circulated by police, Jeremy turned himself in.

After his arrest, Jeremy defended his lack of remorse, arguing that the professional footballers "could afford it."

At the time of the scam, Jeremy was already serving a fourteen-week suspended sentence for posing as a company director in an earlier £14,000 fraud. This time, he was jailed for twenty months, having been charged with three counts of fraud against Pellegrini and Silva, and was ordered to serve the breached fourteen-week sentence on top of that.

Manchester Crown Court heard that the Birmingham resident, at age fifty-six, successfully posed as the thirty-one-year-old Silva, wearing just a cap as a disguise as he withdrew cash from bank machines across Greater Manchester.

Prosecutor Tim Greenald said Silva's bank account had been targeted by a fraudster in September 2015. According to Greenald, an unknown caller pretended to be Silva, calling the bank and passing identity verification controls before ordering a replacement card and a PIN reminder. The card and reminder were allegedly sent to Silva's home, but must have gotten intercepted, as they never arrived. Jeremy then went to four branches of Silva's bank and used the card to make £20,950 in withdrawals.

Pellegrini's account was targeted two days after Silva found out about the missing funds. Again, a con man rang Pellegrini's bank, claiming to be him, passed the bank's security checks and then ordered a replacement debit card, canceling the one Pellegrini held. Somehow, he also obtained Pellegrini's PIN number before intercepting the card. Jeremy then used that card on twenty-three occasions.

Pellegrini, sixty-three, did not even realize that he had been the victim of £130,000 worth of fraudulent withdrawals until he tried to pay for a meal and his card was refused.

Silva and Pellegrini were both reimbursed by their banks. Police are unsure where the stolen money ended up.

JACKNOT!

A winning Canadian lottery ticket was not paid out because it was bought with a stolen credit card, reported the BBC. The Newfoundland woman who allegedly bought the ticket was arrested in January 2019 while on her way to the lottery offices to claim her winnings. Police were following up on a report of a stolen wallet and discovered that the victim's credit cards had been used to buy lottery tickets.

According to the BBC, the thirty-three-year-old suspect was identified with security footage from the store where the tickets were bought. She was taken into custody by officers from the Royal Newfoundland Constabulary and charged with two counts of possessing a stolen credit card and five counts of fraud.

Constable James Cadigan said the amount of the winnings was a "substantial sum."

The Atlantic Lottery Corporation's spokeswoman, Natalie Belliveau, confirmed that the company paid out prizes only for lawfully acquired tickets and said, "Ultimately, if not paid, this amount will go to Atlantic Lottery's unclaimed prize account and will be used for future prizes."

The suspect's bad luck also affected the driver transporting her to the lottery corporation's offices. En route, the driver was ticketed for driving with a suspended license and without insurance, and her vehicle was impounded.

MERCI CRIME

It could have worked.

A Calgary couple had a scheme to defraud their home-insurance company. It was an elaborate plot. They hid their jewelry and electronics, broke windows and faked footprints. Then they called the police to report a robbery.

One of the officers to answer the break-and-enter call that day in June 2010 was Constable Charanjit Meharu. The female "victim" was sobbing and told police she had lost everything valuable in her home. She had prepared a list of the missing things, NPR reported.

Then her father called from Quebec, and she began telling him, in French, what had happened. But it wasn't the same story she had told the police.

What she didn't know was that Meharu, born in India, was fluent in English, Punjabi, Hindi, Urdu, Arabic, Gujarati—and French.

"She was telling him she and her boyfriend had made up the story to make an insurance claim," Meharu said. "By the end, I had about ten pages of notes, and I said, '*Merci beaucoup*.' She didn't expect a brown guy to speak French."

The woman was charged with mischief.

MISS-MAN

This one is a real head-scratcher. *EJ Insight* reported that a Norwegian man was charged for *not* carrying out the murder he was hired to commit. Yes, you read that right. In January 2015, a twenty-one-year-old man was charged with fraud after he agreed to accept money in exchange for killing a specified target. Police discovered the plot, but quickly realized the twenty-one-year-old "hit man" had no intention of ever completing the hit. He was subsequently charged with defrauding his client. The man who ordered the hit was given two years in prison, but his sentence was reduced after he confessed.

We aren't sure what the moral of this story is, but it's probably just that you should never get involved with murder for hire.

FIVE-STAR FAILURE

Perception is everything. Brazen con man "Dennis" was definitely aware of this when he posed as a wealthy businessman and managed to use a canceled credit card to book the Presidential Suite at the Park Regis hotel in Birmingham, England, along with all the perks that came with it: free food, drinks and services, including a gym, a business center and a spa. You know the Presidential Suite is nice, because it was previously used by Hollywood director Steven Spielberg when he was filming in Birmingham.

According to *Metro*, earlier in the year, Dennis had also lived a VIP lifestyle at the AC Hotel in the same city. Birmingham Crown Court heard that Dennis, forty-seven, ran up £124,000 in bills at the two hotels, signing for as much as £700 per day during the spree, from June to December 2016. Staff said he was a generous tipper.

Incredibly, Dennis even posted a review of one of the hotels on his Facebook page during the time of his fraudulent behavior. Sharing a link to the Park Regis official site in October, he wrote, "An amazing staff in an incredible space. Come for lunch and stay for tea." It's safe to say that he was nothing if not committed to the fraud.

Park Regis Birmingham responded to the post, thanking Dennis for promoting the hotel.

Prosecutor Patrick Sullivan told the court that Dennis had posed as a hedge-fund manager who worked for a Swiss bank. He used an HSBC credit card that had been canceled, but persuaded both hotels to employ a rarely used "override" to book in advance. Sullivan said, "He had built up the trust of the people at both hotels. He was very plausible, looked the part, he was a model guest. He tipped the staff well, electronically. He was a platinum-card hotel guest and staff had no idea that he was a fraud."

The hotels only found out about the deception on December 15, when Barclaycard alerted them, reported the *Mirror*.

When Dennis was arrested, police searched his room and recovered the credit card, which had been canceled in July after he had accumulated £90,000 in unpaid charges.

Sullivan said it was unlikely all the money spent at the hotels would be recovered and that the deception had a significant effect on those who worked there. People might even lose their jobs.

The court also heard that Dennis had a previous conviction for a $176,000 fraud relating to a hedge fund in the United States.

Defense lawyer Joseph Keating said Dennis had come to Birmingham because his father was unwell. He noted that Dennis had previously been employed at the managerial level at various companies and was owed £200,000. "His intention was always that the money would be repaid," Keating said.

Dennis admitted two counts of fraud. In passing sentence, the circuit judge told him, "You were utterly manipulative and knew completely what you were doing. You were thoroughly dishonest." Dennis was sentenced to three years and nine months in jail.

THE FRIEND OF YOUR FRIEND IS YOUR FRIEND

It's one of the first things you learn about social media generally, and Facebook in particular: Be careful who you "friend." You don't want people you met for a few minutes at a party, at a bar or on a beach to have access to every aspect of your life.

It's also advisable not to overshare.

"Mathys" was an immigrant to the United States from Cameroon. Between 2003 and 2006, he worked his way up from selling roses in restaurants to massive bank fraud, bilking Seattle credit unions out of over $200,000 with the help of accomplice "Elijah." Elijah and Mathys enlisted fellow conspirators, getting them to apply for car loans with the backing of inflated income statements, and then funneling the money into Elijah's London Autos car dealership and using it to fund an extravagant vacation in Las Vegas.

When Mathys learned that authorities were closing in on him early in 2009, he drove a rental car to Mexico and set up in Cancun. The FBI could not find him.

But then, according to *NBC News*, Secret Service agent Seth Reeg took a gamble and typed Mathys's name into Facebook—and lo and behold, the fugitive popped up. His profile pic showed him in fancy dress, posing in front of a backdrop featuring high-end corporate logos. Unfortunately, all of his settings were private—except for his friends list.

Assistant U.S. Attorney Michael Scoville scrolled through Mathys's "friends" and was astonished to learn that one of them was a former Justice Department official. Scoville messaged the man, requesting a phone call. "We figured this was a person we could probably trust to keep our inquiry discreet," Scoville said.

When they spoke, the former official said Mathys was only an acquaintance, someone he had run into a few times in nightclubs. However, he was able to find out where Mathys was living, and Scoville passed that information on to Mexican police, who quickly placed Mathys under arrest.

Mathys had been living in an apartment complex and working at a hotel—and, of course, partying at Cancun's beaches, pools and nightclubs. When Scoville gained access to his Facebook account, he found updates describing Mathys's days on the beach and nights on the town. "He was making posts about how beautiful life is and how he was having a good time with his buddies," Scoville said. "He was definitely not living the way we wanted him to be living, given the charges he was facing."

Elijah was convicted by a federal jury in Seattle in October 2009 and sentenced the following January in U.S. District Court in Seattle to forty-one months in prison, five years of supervised release and $112,700 in restitution for six counts of bank fraud. It was noted that he had been convicted previously for similar charges.

Mathys was found guilty of four counts of bank fraud and sentenced to thirty-three months in prison.

JUST ANOTHER BRICK IN THE WALL

A software executive was caught putting fraudulent barcodes on Lego toys at Target locations in California and was charged with commercial burglary.

"Tomlin," forty-eight, was sentenced to six months in custody followed by three years on probation. He was also ordered to pay restitution for the stolen goods.

As reported by *Palo Alto Online*, Tomlin targeted four different Target stores between April 20 and May 8, 2012. His scam involved covering the barcode tags of Lego kits with new ones he had created on his computer, allowing him to purchase the toys at a significantly lower cost.

Despite having an excellent job at the time, as a vice president at SAP Labs' Integration and Certification Center (which fired him in September 2012), Tomlin had been boosting his earnings by selling merchandise on eBay since April of 2011. It is unknown whether all of the products were obtained through illegal means, but his Target scam would certainly have improved his profit margins on those items.

Liz Wylie, a Mountain View Police spokeswoman, revealed that Target had video footage of Tomlin making the barcode switches— evidence obtained after the chain's security team became suspicious of his behavior during the first incident. Lego sets are both popular and expensive, and are therefore a draw for thieves, so stores watch them closely.

Tomlin's first "ticket-switching" success was at a Target in Cupertino, California, where he managed to purchase two Lego kits at drastically reduced prices. Later that day, he pulled the same scam at the Mountain View store. He switched the labels on four more sets over the next few weeks, but was eventually recognized by a Target employee who saw him putting the stickers on multiple items, though he purchased only one of them. He was detained by Target security as he left the store, and police arrested him shortly thereafter.

When officers searched Tomlin's gated mansion, they discovered hundreds of toys, still in their packages, including several of the kits stolen from Target. Many of the toys were special-edition items, including Magma Monsters, X-Wing Starfighters and Millennium Falcons.

In an interview reported by *Wired*, Cindy Hendrickson of the Santa Clara County district attorney's office said, "It really looked like a mini Legoland."

For over a year, Tomlin had been selling merchandise on eBay and had sold 2,100 items worth about $30,000. He had 193 items for sale on the e-commerce site at the time of his arrest, most of which were Lego sets, though police were unable to prove that he had purchased those items fraudulently.

"The motive was clearly money," Liz Wylie told *The Mercury News*. "Why does he want the money? I don't know. I can think of a million different possible scenarios. For some people it's boredom. For some it's a compulsive thing."

Tomlin's eBay ratings, by the way, were 99.9 percent positive.

FAKE IT UNTIL YOU MAKE IT?

"Alina" perhaps took the phrase "go big or go home" a little too literally while she was living in New York City. The Russian-born fraudster was charged with multiple counts of attempted grand larceny, theft of services and larceny in the second degree. She had stolen $275,000 from friends and acquaintances while pretending to be a wealthy German heiress with a $60-million trust fund, and had tried to con a bank out of a $22-million loan.

Alina, known also by an alias, was convicted in April 2019 after two days of jury deliberations that followed a six-week trial. In May 2019, she was sentenced in Manhattan Supreme Court to four to twelve years in prison. In addition, Judge Diane Kiesel, who was stunned by Alina's "labyrinth of lies," ordered her to pay $199,000 in restitution and a fine of $24,000.

"I apologize for the mistakes I made," Alina said before she was sentenced.

According to *The New York Times*, Alina was born in Russia on

January 23, 1991, to working-class parents. She moved to Germany with her family in 2007 and, after dropping out of college, immigrated to New York City in 2016. There she created the identity behind her alias, claiming that her father (actually a truck driver) was a wealthy businessman or a diplomat.

"[Alina], who reinvented herself . . . was blinded by the glitter and the glamour of New York City," Judge Kiesel said. "She was [interested] in the designer clothes, champagne, private jets, boutique hotel experiences, and the exotic travel that she thought went along with it, everything that big money could buy. Except [Alina] didn't have big money. All she had was a big scam."

Banks, hotels and a private airline company all made "exceptions" for Alina because they believed she was a German heiress, said her lawyer, Todd Spodek. She tried to get more than $22 million in loans by giving bankers referrals from influential people she had duped into believing she was rich. Alina said she was trying to raise money to open her own social club. Spodek compared her to crooner Frank Sinatra, whose handlers hired fake fans to boost his appeal.

Among the friends Alina was accused of robbing was former photo editor "Renee," who testified that Alina had invited her on an all-expenses-paid trip to Morocco and then stuck her with the $70,000 tab, which she put on her corporate credit card. Renee, thirty-one, cried extensively throughout her testimony, saying she'd had trouble paying rent and credit-card bills after falling victim to Alina's swindle. Renee wrote a long feature article about her experiences with Alina, insisting that she was the victim and wanted to share her story because there were "complex emotions involved."

Renee said in court that the story of her experience with Alina landed her more than $300,000 in book deals and an exclusive-rights deal with HBO.

The *New York Business Journal* reported that Lena Dunham is said to be working on the HBO series about the case, and Shonda Rhimes has announced that she is working on a show about the fake heiress for Netflix.

THERE'S NO PLACE LIKE JAIL!

AN ARRESTED DEVELOPMENT

You might think it would be common sense not to transport stolen property to a police facility when you are being summoned for an unrelated offense. Especially if that police facility is the jail where you are going to serve part of your sixty-day weekend sentence because you are, in fact, already a convicted criminal.

Amazingly, "Jacob," despite having achieved the wise old age of twenty-five, did not know this. And he didn't have the foresight to think through the consequences of driving a stolen car to jail.

He was on his way to Toronto to serve his sentence on an assault charge when he was pulled over by police in Simcoe, Ontario, the *Simcoe Reformer* reported. Jacob was promptly arrested—again.

According to court reports, Jacob later admitted that his first mistake was agreeing to serve his sentence intermittently rather than all at once.

"I thought it was a good idea at the time," he told the courtroom. "I shouldn't have taken that. It was added stress on me. I made the wrong choice."

Jacob claimed he had stolen the car in order to make the drive to Toronto. Presumably, he didn't like taking the bus. The presiding judge, Kevin Sherwood, was quick to point out the flaws in this explanation, most notably that Jacob had been seen using the vehicle four days before he was due in Toronto. It was therefore pretty obvious that he had stolen it for his own enjoyment.

"It's clear from the record, you are not getting the message of deterrence," Sherwood noted.

Jacob's punishment for his errors in judgment was a further ten months in lockup.

THE NOT-SO-GREAT ESCAPE

In September 2017, four inmates of a correctional facility in Mississippi escaped and looted a nearby convenience store. And then, astoundingly, the criminals broke *back into* the prison.

Global News reported that the four men climbed over the prison fence and proceeded on foot to the convenience store, which was closed. They broke in and stole any items they thought they could sell to other prisoners, including cigarettes, lighters and phones. Then they returned to the prison, carrying their stolen goods, and made their way back inside, undetected by guards.

But when Holmes County police reviewed footage from a security camera at the store, they noticed that the robbers were dressed in prison attire. From there, it was easy for them to figure out what had transpired.

All four jailbreakers denied their involvement in the robbery, even though they were videotaped committing the crime. They were charged with commercial burglary.

SWEET DREAMS

There is nothing more important than a good night's sleep. Just ask England's "Keegan," who was sentenced for theft in February 2012. According to *The Telegraph*, Keegan was handed a suspended sentence and a supervision order, meaning that he did not have to serve jail time but had mandatory daily meetings with a probation officer. Some might have seen this sentence as generous. Not Keegan, who found the daily 10 a.m. meetings too early and complained to a judge that they were interfering with his sleep schedule. Keegan even went so far as to ask the judge to send him to prison so that he could "catch up on sleep."

The magistrate told Keegan, "You have failed to co-operate with the requirements of the order. . . . You were given a chance and you have not taken it. Many would say you were fortunate."

The Telegraph reported that Keegan was grinning as he was handed his new prison sentence, and even thanked the judge.

HIJACKERS HAVE THE PISS
TAKEN OUT OF THEM

A DHL courier was confused but eager to help when two women flagged him down in December 2007. They told him they had forgotten to put something in one of the packages he was delivering, and it was crucial that they add it.

As soon as the driver opened the doors to the van, which was transporting urine samples from Crescent City, California, to Eureka for testing by the Department of Justice, the women jumped in and started searching frantically through the urine.

As reported by the *East Bay Times*, the driver heard one of the women say, "I gotta get the stuff or I'll go to prison" as they rummaged through the samples. The driver told them he was calling the police, and the women ran off without finding what they had been looking for.

The two were later identified as a twenty-four-year-old and a twenty-six-year-old, both of whom were on probation and thus subject to regular drug tests. The latter was worried that she'd fail her latest test, which in her case could have resulted in as much as two years in prison. So the two plotted to steal the sample before it could be tested.

But as it turned out, this was harder than it sounded. They had no idea where the sample might actually be. The DHL van was the second one they had tried to search that day; the first had refused to stop.

The bumbling criminals didn't even bother to conceal their identities. Police tracked them down easily and tested both women for drugs. The twenty-six-year-old tested positive for meth. (In an ironic twist, the urine sample they were trying to steal tested clean.)

Del Norte County District Attorney Mike Riese said, "It's one of the more nonsensical crimes I've seen in the twenty years I've been in law enforcement."

The younger woman was sentenced in Del Norte Superior Court to one year in the county lockup for violating probation. The woman who tested positive was sentenced to three years in prison.

"This is about as bold an interference with the drug court process as we have had," Judge Robert Weir said in the court report. "It really takes the cake."

HE'S KNOWN FOR HIS CONVICTIONS

There are repeat offenders, and then there are *repeat offenders*.

In January 2018, fifty-seven-year-old "Rupert" of Miami Beach, Florida, was arrested for the 344th time, this time for standing in the middle of the street with a beer in one hand and marijuana stuffed into his shoe, not incidentally violating a court order that banned him from Miami Beach south of 40th Street.

According to *Local 10 News*, Rupert's previous charges ranged from public drinking and petty theft to strong-arm robbery and sexual battery. He had been convicted five times in the previous twelve months.

In this case, Rupert took a plea deal, avoiding a trial, and was sentenced to ninety days in jail.

Miami-Dade Circuit Court Judge Andrea Ricker Wolfson read him the riot act: "You're on the radar, my friend. Essentially, the officers and the residents who live in that area know who you are, and they will call the police if they see you. And you'll be right back here where you are right now. And I can guarantee you that if you violate the order again, the state won't even discuss a plea with your lawyers."

Miami Beach resident "Jorge" said Rupert's extensive history of arrests and release is just a symptom of a much larger problem. Jorge and some of his neighbors started the Miami Beach Crime Prevention and Awareness Group in 2017, hoping to break the pattern of repeat offenders being arrested and released, and then returning to the beach area. Group members attend court proceedings, hoping to persuade judges to keep offenders like Rupert in custody.

Jorge said he hopes this stint in jail finally sends a message to Rupert and others like him. "Hopefully it'll sink in," he said.

While many in law enforcement support such citizen engagement, Miami-Dade's public defender and the Florida branch of the American Civil Liberties Union have a range of concerns about it, ranging from possible hearsay and/or irrelevant testimony to the possibility of racial profiling and harassment of the homeless.

FACEBOOKED

Convicted thief "Julian," of Oregon, was tired of the court-ordered drug treatment he had agreed to in exchange for not being sent to jail. So he packed up and left.

Feeling liberated by his newfound independence, Julian couldn't help but taunt those he had left behind. He updated his Facebook profile frequently as he drove across the United States. Many of his sneering posts were directed to his probation officer: "Fresh out of another state," he wrote. "Catch me if you can."

In another post, he abandoned discretion entirely: "I'm in Alabama." And he wasn't just trying to lead any pursuers astray—that's where Julian actually was when he was pulled over for speeding. The officer ran his license, found the warrant for his arrest and was more than happy to cut Julian's spontaneous road trip short.

The Oregonian reported that Julian had to reimburse the state $2,600 for his flight back to Oregon and was sent to prison for thirty months.

TAKE ME HOME!

You can take the criminal out of jail, but you can't take jail out of the criminal. At least, that was the case for seventy-three-year-old "William," who had spent forty years behind bars. In fact, William had spent so much of his life in the U.S. prison system that upon getting out, he found that all he wanted was to go back.

So he robbed a bank.

According to *GQ* magazine, William was careful in his planning—to get caught, that is. He made sure to bring a weapon and show it to the teller ("Make sure you put in your report I used a loaded piece. That will give me, what? Twenty more years?" he was quoted saying to police). William made it out of the bank with $4,000; however, he stopped just outside to smoke a cigarette, giving the bank ample time to call police and direct them to him. If that wasn't enough, surveillance cameras show William sitting in his car for a full minute before turning on his engine and driving away.

Unsurprisingly, cops were able to track down the old man rather quickly, and they were baffled when they did and he told them, "Just take me home. I want to go home now."

"Home? You ain't going home!" replied one of the officers. "You just robbed a bank. You're going to jail."

"Yeah . . . that's home," William said.

The detectives who interviewed him were shocked and amused. Detective Joseph Paglia told *GQ*: "I've never had someone thanking me for arresting them so they could go back to prison. I went home that night, I felt good about myself, like I helped the guy out!"

William requested to serve his time at a maximum-security joint, as he was more likely to have friends there and the solitude helped him focus on his painting.

POT-POURRI

A COUPLE OF DOPES

It was like a Harold and Kumar movie, or maybe Cheech and Chong, but it was real life: two guys became so paranoid while getting high that they wound up dialing 911 and turning themselves in.

According to *East Idaho News*, in January 2015, "Lorenzo," twenty-two, and "Horton," twenty-three, were transporting a cargo of weed from California to Montana and had just crossed the Nevada–Idaho border. Unfortunately, they had made the fundamental dope-dealer mistake of smoking a lot of their product. The two men got so high, they became convinced that they were being followed by undercover police (they weren't) and that every car they saw was being driven by cops waiting to bust them but holding off for some unknown reason.

Finally, frantic with worry, they pulled into a gas station in Rexburg, Idaho, and made the 911 call that will go down in history:

"Hi, uh, we're the two dumbasses that got caught trying to bring some stuff through your border, and all your cops are just driving around us like a bunch of jack wagons, and I'd just like for you guys to end it. If you could help me out with that, we would like to just get on with it," Lorenzo told the puzzled dispatcher.

After some more verbal meandering, Lorenzo gave the address of the gas station, said they weren't carrying firearms—the dispatcher asked them about guns "because the undercover cops are just curious"—and added that they only had munchies for the road and a dog, which they were bringing to its owner.

The dispatcher took down the details, by then no doubt realizing how stoned the two men were, and promised to send a nearby marked unit to pick them up.

A police report says the two were arrested without incident. When the responding officers arrived, the two potheads had their hands behind their heads. Horton told the officers, "We got caught and we're surrendering."

Police found 20 pounds of marijuana and some cash in a dog cage in the car, and the two were charged with felony drug trafficking.

Horton was sentenced to five years, but this was knocked down to thirty days because he was a model prisoner. Lorenzo, on the other hand, learned the hard way not to smoke weed, snort cocaine and take oxycodone hours before sentencing, as he tested positive for all of these substances and received one-and-a-half to eight years in prison.

UP IN SMOKE

A Georgia man had little ground to stand on after he was accused of violating his parole by attempting to purchase marijuana. He had, you see, accidentally texted his probation officer instead of his drug dealer.

"You have any weed?" asked the man from Albany, Georgia, in the text message, sent in October 2014. The parole officer showed up at the offender's house with police, who found a bag of cocaine on the premises, *HuffPost* reported.

The misdirected text landed the man one year in prison for violating his probation, plus another year on a drug charge for the cocaine.

DIGGING UP TROUBLE

In 2005, while most eyes were on the criminals transporting contraband from Mexico to the United States, a new route for smuggling marijuana into America was discovered coming from its friendly neighbor to the north.

Canadian authorities became suspicious when they noticed a large amount of lumber disappearing into a small Quonset hut in Langley, British Columbia. They believed it was probable that a tunnel was under construction, the CBC reported. They alerted U.S. authorities, who decided to keep an eye on the area until they knew for sure what was up.

American government agencies, including the FBI and drug enforcement officials, monitored the tunnel's construction for eight months, allowing its completion so they could observe the activities of those constructing it. Investigators even placed cameras and microphones inside the tunnel.

In June 2005, Canadian investigators caught a break. A surveillance team on night watch observed a vehicle driving onto the Langley property, *The Seattle Times* reported. A woman got out and burglarized the Quonset hut, stealing some tools.

Initially, police thought the burglary might compromise their surveillance, but then they decided to capitalize on it and had the woman stopped by police in Abbotsford, British Columbia. During questioning, she described the hut's interior. She had seen tools, a loading ramp, buckets, a hoist and a large piece of plywood covering a hole cut in the cement floor, but no lumber or rebar.

Investigators surmised that all the lumber and rebar they had seen loaded into the hut must be underground, shoring up tunnel walls.

The woman's statements paved the way for search warrants that helped break the case.

Authorities moved in and sealed the tunnel shortly after it opened, in July 2005. The tunnel was 5 feet high, 3 feet wide and 360 feet long, and ended in the living room of an abandoned home in Lynden, Washington, just south of the border. It was extremely well built, reinforced with concrete, iron bars and 2- by 6-inch wood planks. It even had a small cart to transport goods and, perhaps, people. Police said it was the first tunnel they'd ever found along the Canadian border—which was, after all, wide open until 9/11 in 2001.

Three men from Surrey, British Columbia, faced charges in the United States after the discovery of the tunnel, which authorities said was built to transport drugs between Canada and the United States. The men were accused of smuggling 42 kilograms of marijuana through the tunnel and were charged with conspiracy to distribute marijuana and conspiracy to import marijuana.

On Tuesday, February 7, 2006, after six months of negotiations, the three defendants agreed to plead guilty to one felony count each of conspiracy to import marijuana. The sentencing date was set for June 16, 2006, before U.S. District Court Judge John C. Coughenour. After three continuances, sentencing was finally held on July 14, 2006, in a courtroom packed with family members and supporters of the three Canadian prisoners.

According to *The Seattle Times*, Coughenour listened to the three defense attorneys plead for leniency for their clients, and to apologies from the three men, then he sentenced each prisoner to nine years' incarceration, the maximum allowable under U.S. federal sentencing guidelines, and five years of supervised probation upon release from prison. In addition, all seized money and property—the Quonset hut, a truck and $32,000 in cash from one man's bedroom—were forfeited to the U.S. government.

Coughenour said he wanted to send a clear message to Canadians and Americans that trafficking in potent "BC Bud" was a serious crime and violators would be dealt with harshly in U.S. courts.

COPS TO WEED

A twenty-six-year-old man who led police on a high-speed chase through Texas in March 2016 said after the chase that it was a thrill, that he always had pot on him and that he was tired of being persecuted for smoking marijuana.

"Jarod's" road trip started when police tried to pull him over near Dallas and he sped away. It was the beginning of a chase that reached 100 miles per hour. Several law police departments were involved, and at one point thirty patrol cars were in pursuit. Police finally put a stop to the chase around 10:30 p.m. near Waco, Texas, with spike strips on the road and shots fired at the car's tires, causing the vehicle to crash.

"I didn't know they was gonna shoot at me," Jarod told a reporter from *Fox 4* from the back seat of a police car after he was arrested. "I'm like, 'Damn, they shooting at me? I ain't even got no gun!'"

Another reporter asked Jarod if he had weed in the car.

"Yeah, I had weed on me. Yeah. I always have weed on me."

Fox 4 reporter: "Is that why you ran?"

Jarod: "Mm-hmm. I'm tired of getting arrested for weed.... I can't get a regular job ever, anywhere, because of all my weed charges."

Fox 4 reporter: "You said something earlier about the thrill of driving. Was that a thrill?"

Jarod: "It was definitely a thrill. You go fast in any car—race-car track, here—it's fun anywhere. I mean, I'm just an adrenaline junkie."

After the chase, Jarod, a Tennessee resident, was facing charges of evading arrest in a motor vehicle, possession of a controlled substance, possession of marijuana and driving while intoxicated.

"I'm done with people trying to take my freedom because I smoke weed," Jarod told *Fox 4*. "You can drink, it's ten times worse."

HANDS OFF MY WEED!

An Ohio man with a severe case of the munchies called 911 to report that he was "too high on weed" and "could not feel his hands."

NBC's *WFMJ* reported that Austintown police officers responding to the call in October 2015 were directed by the caller's grandfather to an upstairs bedroom, where they heard groaning. The twenty-two-year-old was found lying on the floor, in the fetal position. The police report noted that he was surrounded by "a plethora of Doritos, Pepperidge Farm Goldfish and Chips Ahoy cookies." It was not clear if his groans were due to the marijuana buzz or the triple-snack munchies.

The man, whose name was redacted in the police report, handed over his car keys and gave police permission to search his car, where they found a glass jar of marijuana, rolling papers, a glass pipe with pot residue and two partially smoked joints.

The man refused medical care, and the police decided not to charge him.

SLAM DUNK

One drug dealer had some serious bad luck.

According to a *USA Today* report, a police officer in Morganfield, Kentucky, received calls and texts in June 2018 from people who wanted to buy marijuana from someone named "Dunk."

The officer, Eric McAllister, and a Kentucky state trooper set up a sting operation that caught a fifty-one-year-old suspect and a juvenile. They both told police that Dunk had posted his new number on Snapchat but had apparently mixed up his digits, giving McAllister's number instead of his own.

Police said in a press release that they knew Dunk's real identity, but they did not release it.

USA Today reported that the older man was arrested on several charges, including gun and drug counts. No charges were specified for the juvenile.

PLANTING EVIDENCE

Grow-ops are not such a big deal in certain parts of the world these days, but putting your toddler to bed in the same room as the pot plants is bad. And being caught doing it because you're too wrecked to function is next-level bad.

Metro reported that two British brothers were lucky to avoid prison after they let their children sleep in a house that had been turned into a drug den, and for being too drunk and otherwise under the influence to look after them.

"Damian," twenty-nine, and his brother, "Matt," thirty-five, shared the house in question, in Hull, Yorkshire. Damian went out with friends in July 2017, leaving his three-year-old daughter asleep in a room where he and his brother were growing thousands of pounds' worth of marijuana.

Damian returned home at 4:40 a.m., but passed out in the doorway before he could get inside. A cab driver who spotted him there, and noticed blood on the doorstep, called the police and paramedics.

The police report states that officers entered the house and found Matt asleep in an upstairs bedroom with his two young sons. But it was the next bedroom that revealed the more shocking situation: Damian's daughter and twelve large marijuana plants, worth £6,000 on the street, along with transformers, lights and fans, and a large black ventilation pipe running along the stairs to the front bedroom. The officers smelled cannabis.

Damian, described as drunk and aggressive in the *Metro* report, made it from the front stoop into the living room, where he collapsed on the couch and defecated in his pants.

Police then unsuccessfully tried to awaken Matt.

Megan Rhys, who prosecuted the case at Hull Crown Court in May 2019, told the court that Matt "appeared to be under the influence of something and his speech was slurred. He was seen to be sweating profusely and his skin was pale. He had sweat running from his forehead and was described by a paramedic as 'not being with it.'"

The men and their children were taken to the hospital. Matt, who was supposed to be taking care of his sons and his niece, confessed that he had taken amphetamines and smoked marijuana.

Damian said he and his brother were growing the pot for personal use only. However, both ultimately pleaded guilty to child cruelty by neglect, and Damian admitted being involved in cannabis production.

At the time of the trial, Matt, who had a clean record, had been in custody since March 2019, having missed several court appearances before that date. His lawyer, Richard Thompson, argued that the two months his client had already spent behind bars represented sufficient punishment for his crime.

Damian had previous convictions on his record, but Nigel Clive, speaking in Damian's defense, told the court the young father had only recently reestablished contact with his daughter after not seeing her for eight months. In addition, Damian's new girlfriend was pregnant, and any time behind bars would prevent him from supporting his family

"This is a young man who works and provides for his daughter and will be providing for his new child," Clive said, adding that the incident "was very almost something serious but fortunately none of these children were hurt. This was a one-off occasion."

Circuit Judge Maria Karaiskos scolded the men for their "irresponsible and selfish" parenting, saying, "You both neglected [your children] in a very serious way." She sentenced Damian to twenty days of rehabilitation and 200 hours of volunteer work, and Matt to fifteen days of rehabilitation and 150 hours of volunteer work.

NUMBER ONE WITH A BULLET

It was only a single bullet, but it was enough to put alleged gang member "Darrell," twenty-two, in jail for a year.

In March 2019, U.S. District Court Judge C.J. Williams sentenced Darrell to prison on a charge of being a drug user in possession of ammunition. Court records claim that Darrell is a member of the Del Mob street gang in Waterloo, Michigan.

According to a report by *The Courier*, authorities searched Darrell's home and found a live .40-caliber bullet in a tin can next to his bed. They also recovered marijuana, a digital scale and a piece of shotgun barrel that had been sawed off.

The recovery of the bullet increased Darrell's sentence, but it was to run consecutively with the punishment for his misdemeanor drug charges.

FACE PLANT

SELFIE-MADE MAN

Nineteen-year-old "Randy," of Washington, D.C., kicked in the back door and broke into a reporter's home in December 2011. At first it was a standard heist: he took a nice winter coat, some cash and two laptops, and got away clean. But within a couple of hours, Randy, proud of all he had managed to pull off, couldn't resist logging onto the laptop that belonged to the reporter's son and taking a picture of himself wearing the jacket and flaunting the cash he had taken. Incredibly—and stupidly—he then posted the photo on the son's Facebook page.

Randy's voluntary "mug shot" led to his arrest a month later. Turns out that the Assistant U.S. Attorney prosecuting the case, Sean Lewis, was as adept at using the internet as Randy was inept. With a quick check of the IP address from which the Facebook photo was taken, they had their suspect.

Furthermore, when police caught up with Randy, he was carrying a gun, so in addition to the burglary, he was also charged with carrying a pistol without a license.

One D.C. police officer said Randy was the "most stupid criminal" he had ever encountered, reported the *Daily Mail*.

Upon seeing the evidence for the prosecution that he, himself, had posted, Randy pleaded guilty. He was sentenced to forty-four months in prison on the burglary and weapons charges.

HE THOUGHT HE WAS A GAS

Twenty-year-old "Mitchell" thought it was hilarious when his girlfriend posted a photo on Facebook of him siphoning gasoline from a police squad car. Unfortunately, the police didn't see the humor in the situation.

The photo shows Mitchell, from Jenkins, Kentucky, gesturing with his middle finger while stealing gas from a Jenkins Police Department vehicle. But Jenkins is a small town with only about 2,200 people, and it wasn't long before Mitchell was identified, arrested and charged with theft. He spent the night in jail.

The experience didn't keep Mitchell off Facebook for long, however. As soon as he was released, he posted on his timeline: "yea lol i went too jail over facebook."

According to *CBS News*, Mitchell said there wasn't much gas in the car anyway, and it was all intended as a joke.

But Jenkins Police Chief Allen Bormes believed Mitchell's willingness to steal from police meant he'd steal from "just about anybody."

To prevent future stunts of this nature, the police department added lockable gas caps to its shopping list.

I'LL TAKE ONE WITH EXTRA LETTUCE

A gang of not-so-bright burglars was captured and jailed after they flaunted their stolen money and expensive high-performance cars on Facebook. One gang member even posed with a "cash sandwich": a thick stack of banknotes stuffed between two slices of bread.

The *Daily Mail* reported that, over the course of fifteen robberies between April and September 2012 in the upscale London neighborhoods of Notting Hill, Kensington and Kensal Green, the merry band of burglars stole nine high-end cars, including BMWs, Range Rovers, Porsches and a Mercedes, as well as an assortment of electrical goods and jewelry.

Detectives caught up with the gang after one of them posted a picture of himself on Facebook sitting on the hood of a stolen Range Rover. Police went on to find other incriminating pictures on the social network, along with photos and texts on the gang's telephones bragging about their wealth, posing with stolen cars, drinking champagne, wearing Rolex and Cartier watches and displaying heaps of £20 and £50 notes. Videos showed the men racing the stolen cars and boasting about cars they intended to steal. Police also recovered text messages, sent between the men, planning the burglaries.

After the eight men were arrested in April 2013, burglaries in the Kensington area decreased by 48 percent.

Seven of the eight men pleaded guilty to the burglaries, with one twenty-year-old, described as the "principal conspirator," admitting to his participation in eleven of them. Footage from a police helicopter that showed the man running away from officers was used in court. Another suspect denied taking part, but was ultimately found guilty by the jury.

Prosecutor Mark Paltenghi told Isleworth Crown Court, "It seems quite plain from looking at the evidence that the principal, but not sole aim, was to target houses where valuable cars were kept. Car keys were stolen from the houses and the cars were driven away."

The eight gang members were responsible for stealing hundreds of thousands of pounds' worth of cars. One white Mercedes was particularly coveted by the group. They liked it so much that, even after the car was recovered by police and returned to its owner, the audacious gang tried to use a key they had kept to steal it again, only to find it had been reprogrammed. The attempt was caught on surveillance video, in which the car's owner appears in his boxer shorts to chase the thieves away.

Speaking after the sentencing, one detective inspector said, "Months and months of hard work have finally come to fruition. These eight were a group of young lads who were good at what they did. But their downfall was that they were stupid."

INARTFUL DODGER

For a year, "Rylan," a twenty-five-year-old chef from Poole, England, dodged train fares and gloated about it on Twitter, goading South West Trains and ridiculing its staff in tweets that thanked them for "saving him money." But his "Catch me if you can" taunts finally resulted in the inevitable when he was, in fact, caught.

The tweets began in October 2015, when Rylan, using his personal Twitter handle, posted a picture of customers lining up for tickets with the caption "Look at these muppets buying tickets @SW_Trains." Then he uploaded a selfie taken in first class with the caption "Come get me @SW_Trains first class without a ticket :p."

Later tweets continued the taunting, saying, "Another £4.40 saved thanks @SW_Trains" and "Which first class am I in @SW_Trains coach one or coach 4 #comegetme #noticket."

In one smirking tweet, he bragged that he had "Convinced the aging train assistant he'd already seen my ticket," adding that it was 1–0 in his favor.

He boasted that he was on the rail company's "most wanted list" and advised, "Just no when the ticket man is scoffing a cream cake on carriage 1 if you sit in carriage 4 your home and dry."

When another Twitter user reported him to South West Train's Penalty Fare Support team, Rylan simply retweeted it.

According to *The Telegraph*, the shameless fare dodger was finally caught when a train worker came across Rylan's Twitter page and reported him.

Paul Jones, defending Rylan at Salisbury Magistrates' Court, said his client "could not believe that the tickets were not checked."

Magistrate Simon Browning said it was the worst case of ticket dodging he had ever seen, adding, "You were goading the company on Twitter, and what makes it worse is that you were mocking the staff and putting their photos on Twitter without their permission."

In January 2017, Rylan was ordered to pay the fares for his free rides and fined an additional £1,250—almost twenty-five times the amount of the fares he was convicted of dodging. In addition, he was ordered to perform 120 hours of volunteer work.

We'd say he's learned his lesson.

THANKS FOR YOUR INPUT

Fugitive "Lance" used Facebook to taunt police officers, telling them "Catch me if you can." They did, arresting Lance in the Caerphilly, Wales, area in February 2015, then posted a message of their own on the social media platform: "We would like to thank the public, the media and [Lance] himself for drawing attention to our efforts to return him to prison."

A Facebook user praised the police and commented, "Not so cocky now, is he?"

Another said, "Priceless!! You couldn't write this stuff."

The nineteen-year-old had received an eight-month sentence after being convicted in July 2014 for wounding, affray, common assault and being in possession of a knife. Lance was released from prison while serving that sentence, but his probation was revoked when he failed to attend mandated meetings.

"This demonstrates our commitment to finding and arresting people who fail to abide by the terms of their release from prison," Police Superintendent Marc Budden said.

According to the BBC, earlier that same day, Lance had bragged to a news agency, saying, "They are not going to be able to catch me. I won't let them. They have been round my mum's house four times a day, but I'll be out for at least a month or two before they get me. I have only been out for a week, so I want to be out a bit longer before going back in. I'm still near my home and I haven't seen any police yet. I have been walking around near home so they're not trying too hard to catch me."

So much for that line of thinking.

DISARMED BANDITS

Two men who stole cash from slot machines across Britain were captured after they posted selfies of themselves with their ill-gotten goods.

"Benedict" and "David," from Skegness, Lincolnshire, were sentenced in April 2016 at Bradford Crown Court after pleading guilty to conspiracy to steal, North Yorkshire Police said. Benedict was awarded thirty-two months in prison, while David was given a six-month suspended sentence and 120 hours of community service, reported the BBC.

After one of their hearings, Benedict told reporters outside the court, "I don't care that [I'm] guilty. I'm not bothered, mate. I love it, mate."

Detective Chief Inspector Matt Walker told press the men were stopped for speeding in June 2015 near Skipton, North Yorkshire. A search of the car found more than a thousand £1 coins and £2,000 in notes, as well as balaclavas and a screwdriver.

A police spokesman said David, twenty-four, and Benedict, twenty-nine, wore balaclavas during their thefts, but took them off when they photographed themselves celebrating, posing and grinning with the cash.

Detective Chief Inspector Matt Walker said, "We knew we hit the jackpot when we investigated these lemons."

HE ROBBED THEM THE WRONG WAY

If you're planning to rob a place, it's best not to post about your intentions on Facebook.

You'd think that wouldn't need saying. But the *Mirror* reported that "Anson," thirty-two, of Gaywood, England, was sentenced in Norwich Crown Court to four years in prison and an additional four years on parole after posting a picture of a knife on his Facebook page in February 2015 and writing, "Doing. Tesco. Over." Fifteen minutes after the post was made, police caught Anson with a knife and £410 stolen from a Tesco in King's Lynn, Norfolk.

Judge Anthony Bate, during sentencing, said Anson posed a "high risk of serious harm to the public."

"It was a bizarre and unusual case," said Sergeant Pete Jessop.

The arrest came about after a member of the public reported seeing a man with a knife demanding cash from staff at the Tesco.

In his escape from the supermarket, Anson stole a car from a couple who had stopped to use an ATM, but he fled only as far as a nearby pub.

Jessop said Anson's Facebook confession made it easier to secure a guilty plea. "The pictures and posts on Facebook helped us confirm what we already knew," said Jessop. "None of this takes away from the seriousness of the crime or the trauma experienced by the victims."

Anson also admitted carrying a knife as an offensive weapon.

LOGGING TIME

There's dumb, and then there's the kind of dumb where you leave yourself logged into Facebook on a computer at the house you just robbed.

In October 2009, Italian police nabbed a thief after he couldn't resist checking Facebook while carrying out a burglary in Albano Laziale, near Rome. According to *The Telegraph*, officers noticed the computer was still on. When the fifty-two-year-old homeowner brought the computer to life, the social network site's homepage came up. The victim told the officers he wasn't on Facebook, and they soon realized that the burglar had used the computer and forgotten to log off.

The thief was very active on Facebook, having updated his status several times over the course of a few days, and police were able to easily trace him and recover the stolen goods.

Major Ivo Di Blasio, of the *carabinieri* paramilitary police, said: "He was tempted to log on during the break-in and it led to his arrest. It was a silly mistake to make and we were onto him very quickly. He did not expect us at all and was very surprised when we told him how we had tracked him down. He has a history of break-ins and will now go before a judge."

THAT REALLY STINGS

A CASE OF BEER

Police forces all over the world prefer to trick wanted people into giving themselves up. It's expensive to find them and take them in, so it's much better all around if you can get the bad guys to come to you.

One of the most popular stings is called the "warrant roundup," which involves offering prizes to people who have open arrest warrants. When the wanted person shows up to claim their prize, they get arrested instead.

One such roundup involved beer. As reported by *The Telegraph*, in September 2013, police in Derbyshire, England, sent letters to a number of wanted people they'd had difficulty capturing, saying the outlaws had been selected by a marketing company to receive a case of free beer. When the fugitives called the phone number in the letter, they were directed by undercover officers to meet at a certain time and place to pick up their prize. A total of nineteen dangerous criminals were handcuffed and taken off the street.

Chief Inspector Graham McLaughlin, who led the sting, known as Operation Rocky, believed the ruse was more effective than traditional methods. "These suspects are people who have managed to evade arrest for some time, so we have used different tactics to find them," he said. "It has been very cost-effective, as it can take a lot of time and money to track people down."

Those arrested had been charged with offenses including burglary, robbery and sexual assault.

XBOX 360S

In 2007, the El Paso, Texas, police force, aided by federal U.S. Marshals and the Lone Star Fugitive Task Force, came up with a plan to catch some of the state's most wanted criminals. According to *Wired*, they sent out messages telling the lawbreakers that they had won Xbox 360s and big-screen TVs. All they had to do was show up and walk away with an up-to-date gaming system. But rather than getting gaming gear, 115 fugitives were arrested, clearing 129 warrants.

TVs

Who would believe that companies were giving away free televisions? More than 100 fugitives in Cook County, Georgia, apparently. The sting, called Operation C.W. Marketing, started with police sending out letters to 10,000 people with outstanding warrants. The letters informed the alleged criminals that they could get free electronics just for trying them out. When the respondents pulled up to the warehouse rented by the police department, *CBS Chicago* reported, undercover officers greeted them with big smiles and boxes of home entertainment gear. But then they were brought inside and told they were under arrest.

METH CHECK

In March 2016, the Granite Shoals Police Department posted an advisory on Facebook: "If you have recently purchased meth or heroin in Central Texas, please take it to the local police or sheriff department so it can be screened with a special device. DO NOT use it until it has been properly checked for possible Ebola contamination!" So, as reported by NBC's *WKYC 3*, a twenty-nine-year-old Texas woman went to the Granite Shoals PD to have her meth checked. But she came away charged with criminal possession of less than 1 gram of a controlled substance.

FOOTBALL TICKETS

When the Auburn, Alabama, police department wanted to catch parents who were tens of thousands of dollars behind on their child-support payments, they lured them in with the irresistible story that they had won tickets to the Iron Bowl, the big annual football game between the Auburn Tigers and the Alabama Crimson Tide. According to a report from *HuffPost*, when the negligent parents showed up at the address given, they were handed tickets and congratulated for being "winners," but when they were escorted to the next room, they were handcuffed and told what was really going on. One of those arrested didn't understand the concept, asking, "Do I still get my tickets?"

UNUSUAL SUSPECTS

HE ROBBED HIS FIRST BANK
AT EIGHTY-SEVEN, AND
ANOTHER, AND ANOTHER

In December 1998, J.L. Hunter "Red" Rountree decided to rob a bank. So a week before his eighty-seventh birthday, he did just that, becoming—as far as anyone knows—the oldest active bank robber in the world at the time, and something of an American folk hero.

The son of a farmer, Rountree was born on December 16, 1911. In the early 1930s, he hitchhiked to Arlington, Texas, to enroll at agricultural college. According to *GQ*, he eventually set up the Rountree Machine Company, which manufactured cable winches for offshore oil rigs. The business flourished, and when Rountree sold it in the 1970s, it fetched $1 million.

But then he invested in a shipyard, which did not flourish, and when a bank called in a loan, it bankrupted him. He resented banks for the rest of his life. Rountree's stepson died in an automobile accident, and 1986 brought the death of his wife, Fay, whom he had married in 1936.

At the age of seventy-six, Rountree married a thirty-one-year-old drug addict he met in a bar, began using heroin and cocaine, and spent $500,000 on rehab programs before he and his wife divorced two years later, *GQ* reported.

By the time he was eighty-seven, he felt like he had nothing to lose, and he still hated banks.

"You want to know why I rob banks?" he said. "It's fun. I feel good, awful good."

Rountree kicked off his bank-robbing career at the Southtrust Bank in Biloxi, Mississippi. He was arrested almost immediately, and was convicted and given a three-year suspended sentence, as well as a fine of $260, and told to leave the state.

His second robbery was at Nations Bank in Pensacola, Florida. He was again caught and convicted, this time receiving a sentence of three years in prison.

After he got out, he tried to live a straight life, but he couldn't resist robbing another bank at the age of ninety-one. In August 2003, Rountree walked into the First American Bank in Abilene, Texas, and handed a large envelope marked "Robbery" to the teller. The teller said, "Are you kidding?"

It was his third bank holdup in five years, and it was no more successful than the first two. Leaving the bank, he drove off in a 1996 Buick Regal with nearly $2,000 in small bills. But a witness had noted his license number, and he was arrested half an hour later when he was pulled over after a 90-mile-per-hour chase. By the time he was caught, he had forgotten why he wanted to rob the bank, the *Los Angeles Times* reported.

This robbery earned him twelve-and-a-half years in prison. He died at the U.S. Medical Center for Federal Prisoners in Springfield, Missouri, on October 12, 2004.

HIT AND RUN

Leo Tolstoy famously said, "Happy families are all alike; every unhappy family is unhappy in its own way."

The family of "Jack," a former professor at the Massachusetts Institute of Technology (you know, where smart people go to school), could not have been any unhappier, and their unhappiness was unique in many ways. All but one of his children joined forces to sue for legal separation from him, and the one who didn't said, "What we have learned about Dad is monstrous, and we should have nothing to do with him."

According to a report from *The Guardian*, Jack taught at MIT for nearly thirty years, wrote books, gave lectures, founded several tech companies and amassed an estimated fortune of $100 million. He refused to pay contractors for work done; sued and was sued by a wide range of colleagues, business partners and, especially, his own adult children, over family businesses, inheritances and property; and was accused of extortion and child molestation. (He has said that the daughter who accused him of molesting her was stealing from a family company.)

Aside from the legal-separation suit, Jack's children also filed a restraining order against him. He forged documents and doctored recordings to advance his own interests, and—notoriously—shot himself in the stomach in an effort to implicate one of his sons in a phony hit, supposedly by Russian assassins.

In investigating the "hit," police found that Jack had altered the angle of a surveillance camera so that it wouldn't record him shooting himself in the parking lot of his company in December 2005. Video footage taken a few days before the "attack" showed Jack redirecting a security camera in the parking lot. Jack fired his rifle four times, once at his minivan's door and three times at his own abdomen.

Police discovered a to-do list in Jack's pocket when they responded to his 911 call. The detailed plan for the plot was written on the dinner menu of the Algonquin Club, to which he belonged.

In the 911 call, Jack accused his son of hiring Russian hit men to kill him and laundering $180 million.

In August 2007, Jack was sentenced to two years on probation and ordered to pay a $625 fine and perform 200 hours of community service. The judge also ordered Jack to stay away from his four eldest children and their families.

Middlesex Superior Court Judge Kenneth Fishman said, "[Jack]'s behavior . . . can be described as nothing short of bizarre and premeditated."

It just goes to show: even if you're smart, you can be dumb.

YEAH, THAT'S THE TICKET

Three men, including a prominent sports-radio personality, were sentenced for conspiring in a multimillion-dollar ticket fraud scheme. Disgraced radio host/commentator "Chris," who used to cohost a popular morning show on WFAN and CBS Sports Network, was sentenced to forty-two months in prison in Manhattan federal court in April 2019, according to the *Chicago Tribune*. Strip-club manager "Morty" was given twenty-one months for his involvement in the scheme.

Chris, Morty and a third man were all convicted of defrauding people who invested in a ticket reselling business. The latter was already serving a seventy-eight-month prison term after pleading guilty to securities fraud in October 2017.

As well as ripping off investors, Chris and Morty would promise victims VIP tickets to sporting events and concerts, but would never produce the tickets. You have to wonder how long they thought they could pull off these scams without someone noticing.

Nevertheless, as *The New York Times* reported, the three conspirators took in more than $7 million from investors and ticket-buyers, and used millions of those dollars to pay off other investors and their own personal expenses, including $600,000 for Chris's gambling debts, which he blamed on an addiction to betting.

Chris told U.S. District Court Judge Colleen McMahon, "Putting me in prison accomplishes nothing. It doesn't make society a safer place. It makes me disappear."

In asking for leniency, he said, "Should you show me that mercy, you will not regret it."

Chris, who was convicted in November 2018 of securities fraud, wire fraud and conspiracy, faced up to forty-five years in prison, but got far less time because of federal sentencing guidelines.

Morty wept as he asked the judge for leniency, saying he was led astray by Chris. "He radiated energy and a drive that drew me in," Morty said of the broadcaster. "I was a bit awed and flattered. I went into the ticket business because I believed in [Chris]. . . . I allowed myself to be blinded by him. For too long a time, I just didn't question him."

"There is no difference between what you did and what Bernie Madoff did except the scale of it," McMahon said, according to the *New York Post.*

The *Chicago Tribune* reported that the judge did not believe Chris when he said he hadn't intended to squander the investments, saying, "The money always runs out at some point and only then do you realize the road to your personal hell was truly paved with your good intentions."

FOR OLD-TIMER'S SAKE

Okay, so this particular perp wasn't "dumb," certainly, nor was she actually a criminal, but she did manage to get herself arrested.

"Alice" was picked up by police as part of a bucket-list wish program. As the *Daily Mail* reported, the retired secretary had filled out a wish form, saying, "My wish is . . . to be arrested. I am 104 and I have never been on the wrong side of the law."

Alice, a resident at Stokeleigh Care Home in Stoke Bishop, Bristol, in southwest England, was "detained" by two officers in March 2019 as part of the Wishing Washing Line, a charity initiative in which care home residents' wishes are hung up on a clothesline at local stores, the idea being that shoppers reading them might be able to turn a dream into reality.

Alice's wish came true when Police Constable Stephen Harding and Police Community Support Officer Kelly Foyle arrived at her care home one morning, placed her under arrest and escorted her to their police car for a ride.

Alice said afterward that she'd enjoyed her time with the officers. "I had a lovely day. It was interesting. Nothing like that ever happened to me before. They put the handcuffs on, I had the lot. What did it feel like being a criminal? Well, it will make me much more careful of what I say and do. But the police were very nice throughout."

She also appreciates the care she gets at the home, where she has lived for ten months. "I get to do a lot of different activities here—I have a go at everything, and they're very nice to me."

PCSO Foyle said the actual arrest was handled by her colleague PC Harding. "As far as I know she's the oldest person he's arrested. She was smiling, she had a lovely time.... She did come quietly, and she wanted to be handcuffed so we very gently applied the handcuffs and escorted her down to the police car."

Simon Bernstein, the chief executive of Alive Activities, which runs the Wishing Washing Line initiative, told the *Daily Mail*, "Our charity provides lots of creative activities for older people and engages the community in coming into care homes."

The project originated in Essex, where thousands of wishes have been fulfilled. "It can be as simple as going to the pub for a pint or having somebody to knit with or play bridge with, it can be anything," Bernstein said. "One man said he wanted to see Elvis, but you can't make every wish come true."

According to the Stokeleigh care home manager, other residents have also posted their wishes: "One resident wished to have bikers come here and rev the engines, one would like to go in a Rolls Royce and have a ride, and another resident would like to drive a car because he never has."

No more arrest wishes, however.

THAT'S NOT WHAT DRIVE-THRU MEANS

In January 2010, a ninety-one-year-old resident of Daytona Beach, Florida, and a doting husband, drove his ninety-year-old wife to the beauty parlor. Then, according to *Fox News*, he decided to get some breakfast at the Biscuits 'N' Gravy & More restaurant in Port Orange while he was waiting for her. So he drove to the diner.

Regrettably, he also drove *into* the diner through the front window, knocking aside tables and injuring one of the customers.

Then, as one does, he sat down and ordered breakfast.

"I ordered that after about an hour," the man said in an interview. "I was pretty shaken up."

The breakfast, he said, "was really good," and the staff at Biscuits 'N' Gravy "were wonderful to me and I will go back."

He added that he was glad he got his wife to the beauty parlor first. "She looks great," he said. "We both look great."

The driver himself suffered no injuries, but he received a citation for reckless driving.

HOW THE TABLES
HAVE TURNED

DISCOUNT BEATING

There are a lot of variables that are hard for a robber to plan for in advance. One wannabe store robber would testify to this after he was beaten up by an angry bystander with a baseball bat while attempting to hold up a thrift store in Fells Point, Maryland, in 2009.

"Mike," described as a "career criminal," was sentenced in November 2011 to twenty years in federal prison after a jury convicted him of robbery, the *Daily News* reported.

During his sentencing hearing, prosecutors said Mike, forty-one, had targeted Killer Trash on Broadway three times in eight days. They added that Mike had committed another fourteen robberies in the span of a month, using a collapsible wooden yardstick covered in tape and wrapped in a plastic bag to resemble a firearm.

Federal authorities believed their strongest evidence involved the thrift shop—police had matched Mike's DNA to a baseball cap and $4 he had taken from the thrift shop but had left behind after the beating—so they focused their efforts on that case. But prosecutors used information about the other robberies to influence sentencing.

"I don't regret it at all," said the bystander, who testified at Mike's trial and said in 2009 that he had gotten "about three or four clean shots at his head" with the baseball bat. "I'm happy he got what he got," said the witness, regarding Mike's sentence.

He said at the trial that he attacked Mike to protect his girlfriend, the store clerk, rather than as a vigilante. Trial testimony showed that Mike had grabbed the clerk's throat and pushed her into a clothing rack during the holdup.

The clerk still works at Killer Trash. "It was absolutely terrifying," said the twenty-three-year-old, who helped her boyfriend beat the suspect by hitting him with a jewelry bag. "It was intimidating to see him again in the courtroom. But there's a part of you that says you have to stick up for yourself. I couldn't back down out of fear. This store is my livelihood. I'm not going to let somebody bully me out of my life."

The suspect was described in court papers as a destitute ninth-grade dropout who, in the summer of 2009, terrorized a string of business owners in several Baltimore areas: Fells Point, Charles Village, Mount Vernon and downtown. Among the targets, according to police, was the Lutheran Mission Society Compassion Center, a hand-me-down spot.

In 2006, Mike was convicted of robbing the same Subway sandwich shop three times in eight days (seems like a pattern with him), but his twenty-one-year sentence in that case was substantially reduced on appeal because of errors in the trial.

Prosecutors said Mike never got much from his heists—a total of $4,500 from fourteen robberies in 2009, and nothing from his three attempts at Killer Trash. His spree at Subway in 2006 netted a total of $510, which police said he spent on drugs.

80,000 ANGRY BEES

A burglar's attempt to steal tools and machinery from Potters Fields Park in London, England, was foiled when he accidentally knocked over four bee hives, releasing 80,000 angry bees.

Dale Gibson, an award-winning beekeeper and the creator of Bermondsey Street Bees in Potters Fields Park, told the press that the thief had attempted to scale the fence and, in doing so, fell and landed on the hives. He believes that when the hives were overturned, the bees launched into a "defensive response" that prompted them to chase after the thief.

"Although they can't see in the dark," Gibson said in an interview with the *Evening Standard*, "bees can find enough reason to go three feet and drive off attackers. That's how they would have viewed the incursion by our would-be burglar. It meant that nothing was stolen, no locks were tried, and presumably the person who jumped down was pretty inclined to jump up again . . . but not without having an up-close moment with agitated bees that really meted out their own form of insect justice.

"The hives were able to be put back together and we didn't lose any honey stock, but we did have some casualties. I think the bees would have given as good as they got."

Gibson added that he was "exasperated" by what had happened, which he described as "beyond reckless."

Neither Gibson nor Potters Fields Trust, a nonprofit organization that manages the park, reported the February 25, 2019, incident to the police, and Gibson believes "natural justice has been served."

MAYBE THEY PICKED
THE WRONG GUY

In July 2017, St. Henri, Quebec, resident Joshua Harley was walking home from work on a bike path along the Lachine Canal when he was accosted by muggers.

"Two guys asked me for money for the bus," Harley said. "I reached into my pocket, and I had a $20 bill in there and a toonie and a loonie [two- and one-dollar coins, for non-Canadians] and a couple of quarters, and one of the two strongly suggested that I just give him all the money I had on me. It kind of escalated from there."

Unfortunately for the robbers, they picked on the wrong guy. Harley was not only a martial arts instructor; he also competed as a mixed martial arts fighter. So, in a surprising turn of events for the muggers, Harley fought back. He grabbed the closest man and knocked him to the ground, prompting the other man to flee—as did the one on the ground when he regained his feet.

"I have a black belt in karate," Harley said. "I've done Muay Thai for seventeen or eighteen years, I've fought professionally in Muay Thai and mixed martial arts, so I've been around the block."

According to *CTV News Montreal*, Harley then called the police and explained what had happened. He described the men as in their thirties, white with brown hair, and with Quebecois accents. One was in a black T-shirt, the other in a motorcycle vest with no patches.

Fighting back is not an approach Harley recommends for everyone, but it's pretty much what he does for a living. "I could've just as easily got hurt. I mean, if someone pulled a knife or a weapon, I could have been in deep, deep trouble," he said. "It's not worth getting killed over $24 and a pack of gum."

Harley said better lighting is needed around the canal, and police should increase foot patrols in the region. But police say walking on the street is a safer option. "If you can walk on the street it's better for you," Officer Sylvain Parent said. "The lighting is more persistent, there are more people. If people feel safe going on the bike path, it's okay for them, but one thing is for sure—we won't be able to take our car at night and patrol the bike path."

EARLY RETIREMENT

An eighty-three-year-old British retiree chased off a serial burglar in July 2016 when she discovered him sitting in her Newcastle living room. He fled when she confronted him, but was caught from above on CCTV surveillance cameras. As reported by the *Mirror*, police were easily able to identify the man because the bald patch on his head was so distinctive.

The suspect, who was forty-four at the time, walked into the victim's house in broad daylight after strolling along a laneway behind the house and entering through the first unlocked door he came to.

The elderly woman heard a noise in another room and went to check it out, only to find the man sitting in her living room. When she demanded to know what he was up to, he ran. He did not, apparently, have time to steal anything.

When he was arrested, the intruder claimed he had just been looking for his dog, but his rap sheet would seem to contradict that. He had spent most of the previous decade in prison for burglary, the *Mirror* reported. He had numerous previous convictions for break-ins, including a four-year sentence in 2013 for burgling another elderly person by tricking his way into the house.

The man was sentenced to forty months in jail after admitting the burglary.

DISARMING

In November 2018, a knife-wielding man tried to rob a convenience store in Dongguan City, China. The store's owner, however, fought off the armed criminal, administering a terrific beating in the process, while his wife called the police.

The thief, whose plan was definitely going awry, was knocked unconscious by the end of the one-sided fight, and the storekeeper held him until the cops arrived.

According to the *New York Post*, which posted a video of the incident on YouTube, both combatants were treated for minor injuries at a nearby hospital, and the knife-wielding suspect was arrested.

GOOD EVENING, OFFICER

An attempted carjacking in Chicago was thwarted by the intended victim in June 2018. Two armed men got into a parked BMW, apparently hoping to threaten the driver into leaving so they could steal his car. But unbeknownst to the carjackers, the driver was an armed off-duty police officer, and he wasn't about to let anyone leave with his vehicle. He exchanged gunfire with the would-be car thieves, who were last seen fleeing—on foot.

THIS JOB IS MURDER

INCOMING!

"Quigley" of Gaithersburg, Maryland, was in jail awaiting trial for a serious crime, and it looked like the prosecution had a really good case: a witness who had helped him plan the offence was willing to testify, and Quigley's cell phone records showed that he was in the area at the time. On top of that, the night before the crime, Quigley had announced his intentions to friends.

According to *The Frederick News-Post*, Quigley's lawyer thought the case against him was so strong, he was advising his client to plead guilty.

But Quigley had another plan. He knew the jail authorities didn't check prisoners' outgoing mail, so he wrote a letter to a friend in Washington, D.C., urging him to threaten two witnesses. In fact, he wrote two such letters. But he got his friend's address wrong, and the letters were returned to sender, *The Washington Post* reported. Jail authorities *always* check incoming mail for contraband, and they found Quigley's solicitation to intimidate witnesses, which they promptly forwarded to the Maryland State Attorney's office.

Quigley was segregated from the jail's general population and lost his letter-writing privileges. Jail officials later caught him trying to slip a note to another inmate to mail.

Quigley was subsequently charged with three new counts, which were added to his original charges.

As reported by *The Washington Post*, nearly two years later, in August 2007, a jury found Quigley guilty on all counts.

RELAX, STAY A WHILE, GET CAUGHT

A series of holiday selfies posted to a social media website led Chinese police right to a fugitive hit man.

The man, identified only by the surname Qin, had been in hiding for a year after failing to kill one of his targets in China's Henan Province.

According to *The Statesman*, during the three-day May Day holiday, Qin appeared on the popular Chinese messaging and photo-sharing website WeChat, posting selfies taken on Wudang Mountain in Hubei Province, just south of Henan.

The photos came to the attention of the police in Wudang Mountain, who quickly located Qin by identifying the photos' backdrops and arrested him shortly thereafter.

Qin told police that he had joined a group of friends on the mountain tour because he needed a vacation. Furthermore, because he believed that "the most dangerous place is the safest," he registered in a luxury hotel next door to the police station.

He said he had posted the selfies because the holiday had made him unworried about being wanted by the police.

Logic doesn't seem to be Qin's strong suit.

THE AUTHOR OF
HIS OWN MISFORTUNE

In 2003, Polish photographer "Kristof" wrote and published a crime novel titled *Amok*, which quickly became a bestseller. The tale of torture and murder was well publicized and captured the imagination of the Polish people. However, according to *The Guardian*, it also captured the attention of the police, who found that the story told in the book closely resembled the actual unsolved abduction, torture and murder of Wroclaw businessman and advertising executive "Dmitri."

Chillingly, the novel included details that only Dmitri's killer could know, so investigators took another look at the cold case and discovered that not only had Kristof known Dmitri, but he was the last person to have seen the victim alive. After the businessman's death, Kristof actually sold Dmitri's mobile phone.

The police built a strong enough circumstantial case against Kristof to bring it to trial, where the prosecution argued that the killing had been a crime of passion committed because Kristof believed Dmitri was having an affair with his ex-wife. Both experts and witnesses told the court that Kristof was a sadistic man and a control freak. He believed he was extraordinarily intelligent, and wanted everyone around him to think so too.

The district court in Wroclaw heard that Dmitri's body had been found by fishermen in the Oder river in December 2000, four weeks after he went missing. The victim had been stripped, tortured, bound and dumped in the river. But there was little evidence to assist the police in their inquiry, and they dropped the case six months after the body surfaced, according to *Time*.

Five years later, Commissar Jacek Wroblewski received a tip advising him to read Kristof's grisly novel. He did, and noted the similarities between the fictional murder and the one he had investigated in real life. In the thriller, the narrator, Chris, gets away with murder; Wroblewski was determined that Kristof would not be so lucky. He arrested Kristof, who was known to occasionally go by Chris, and held him for three days before being forced to release him due to lack of evidence. But Wroblewski was sure Kristof was the killer, and when more circumstantial evidence was found, he arrested him again.

Throughout his trial, Kristof maintained that the details in his book had come from news reports about Dmitri's murder. But despite his protestations of innocence, he was convicted, and, in September 2007, given twenty-five years in prison. In sentencing Kristof, Judge Lidia Hojenska said that, although there was a dearth of direct evidence, "The evidence gathered gives sufficient basis to say that [Kristof] committed the crime of leading the killing of [Dmitri]."

"He was pathologically jealous of his wife," Hojenska continued. "He could not allow his estranged wife to have ties with another man."

The case drew widespread media coverage in Poland and resulted in increased sales for the novel, *The Guardian* reported.

In 2007, after Kristof's imprisonment, an appeals court ordered a new trial. In December 2008, he was found guilty again and continued to serve his twenty-five-year sentence.

Kristof is said to be working on a second novel, tentatively titled *De Liryk*. Police report finding evidence on his computer of plans to kill a new victim as a tie-in with the new book.

POLLY WANTS A WITNESS

B ud, an African gray parrot, found himself a key witness in the arrest of "Glinda," a forty-nine-year-old resident of White Cloud, Michigan, who was accused and convicted of murdering her husband, "Melvin." Melvin was shot five times in May 2015. When police arrived at the scene, they found Glinda with a head wound that prosecutors later said was a suicide attempt.

CBC Radio reported that the investigation of the shooting dragged on for a year before Melvin's first wife, who inherited Bud, made public a videotape of the parrot imitating two people having an argument, including the repeated words "Don't [expletive] shoot."

Although it may seem like a stretch that a parrot could produce distinct and recognizable voices, this is, in fact, one of their recognized abilities. In an interview with *Live Science*, Dr. Irene Pepperberg, a researcher at Harvard University, reported that parrots have more muscles in their throat than other birds, allowing them not only to create sounds that mimic human speech, but also to replicate the inflection and pitch of human sounds. Pepperberg says it is common for parrots owned by couples to "switch back and forth between registers to imitate husband and wife." This report lends a lot of credibility to the first wife's claim.

A mere three weeks after the videotape was released, Glinda was charged with first-degree murder and a felony firearms offense. Police believe money issues led to a fight between the couple, pointing to the couple's gambling and the fact that their home was in foreclosure. In July 2017, a Newaygo County jury found her guilty, and she was sentenced to life in prison.

I DO CONFESS

When prisoner "Jordan" had a heart attack in 2009, he thought he was going to die. So he got the attention of the nearest person, a prison guard, and said, "I have to get something off my conscience."

He had beaten a woman to death in Nashville, Tennessee, in 1995, he told the guard. The guard, of course, reported the confession, and prosecutors moved to indict Jordan and bring him to trial, *ABC News* reported.

Jordan, who was serving an unrelated fifteen-year sentence for a 2006 attempted second-degree murder, later recovered from his heart troubles and tried to recant the confession, but to no avail. Prosecutors used his confession, along with evidence from 1995, and took him to trial.

The victim was a thirty-five-year-old Nashville woman who had been found dead by firefighters inside an abandoned home. She had been stabbed, beaten with a cinder block, rolled in a rug and set on fire.

Authorities had suspected Jordan of being the murderer, but a lack of evidence had barred them from pressing charges.

"There was indication that [Jordan] had known her for some time," Susan Niland, with the Davidson County District Attorney General, told *ABC News*. "It was enough where they spent time together. They may have had a sexual relationship."

In October 2012, Jordan was convicted for the 1995 murder and sentenced to fifty-one more years in prison.

MISCELLANEOUS
MAYHEM

MADE IN CHINA

Feeling stressed at work? An American man has the solution: just hire a company in China to do all your work, pay them a fraction of what you are paid and reap the benefits. Seriously.

A security audit on a U.S. critical infrastructure company in 2012 revealed that one of the staff members had been outsourcing his job to China. According to the official report, the software developer, a man in his forties, spent his workdays surfing the web, watching cat videos on YouTube and browsing Reddit and eBay while a Chinese software consultancy was logging in to the company's server to do the programmer's work remotely.

He reportedly paid a fifth of his six-figure salary to a company based in Shenyang, in northwest China, to do his job.

Verizon, which conducted the audit, said the scam came to light after the firm noticed anomalous activity on its virtual private network (VPN), specifically that the traffic logs for its best programmer showed a regular series of logins to the company's main server from Shenyang, *The Next Web* explained. The company suspected that malware had been used to route confidential information from the company to China.

Verizon's Andrew Valentine said the infrastructure company asked the auditor's risk team to investigate the activity. The open and active VPN connection from Shenyang to the employee's workstation went back months, Valentine said. Furthermore, the employee's credentials had been used to start and maintain the VPN connection from China.

"Authentication was no problem," Valentine told *ABC News*. "He physically FedExed his [security] token to China so that the third-party contractor could log in under his credentials during the workday. It would appear that he was working an average nine-to-five work day."

A check of the employee's computer revealed hundreds of invoices from the Shenyang contractor.

The employee, an "inoffensive and quiet" but talented man versed in several programming languages, "spent less than one-fifth of his six-figure salary for a Chinese firm to do his job for him," Valentine said. "Evidence even suggested he had the same scam going across multiple companies in the area. All told, it looked like he earned several hundred thousand dollars a year, and only had to pay the Chinese consulting firm about $50,000 annually."

According to *ABC News*, the employee no longer works at the firm.

DIALING IT IN

A stealthy pickpocket managed to swipe almost twenty cell phones over the course of a Korn and Limp Bizkit concert at England's Manchester Arena in December 2016.

"Sorin's" fatal mistake was not being satisfied with a bounty of nineteen phones. The victim of his twentieth attempt, realizing what Sorin was trying to do, contacted security, and police used surveillance videos to track Sorin through the arena, according to an *ITV News* report.

"Thanks to the immediate reporting of an unsuccessful theft and a detailed description, we were able to arrest Sorin as he was leaving the venue," Detective Constable Richard King of the British Transport Police said. "This meant we retrieved the haul of mobile phones and have so far managed to return fifteen to their owners."

Sorin, a Romanian national, was sentenced to three months in jail and was to be deported after serving his sentence.

AIN'T TOO PROUD TO BEG

District Judge Barney McElholm, of Londonderry, Northern Ireland, warned that professional street beggars were taking advantage of the "generous and good nature of the local people in this community." He made this comment in March 2019 while sentencing a thirty-year-old Romanian woman to two months in prison for stealing a bottle of vodka.

McElholm believed the defendant was "a member of a professional gang of street beggars who could afford to fly into and out of Northern Ireland every six weeks, on a shift basis, to beg," the BBC reported.

McElholm said, "I don't believe a single word of what she has said and I am going to take a tough line in such cases in future."

He added, "I know what help is offered to genuine homeless people ... and if they are truly indigent they would receive offers of support. These people are doing a great disservice to people who are genuinely homeless."

McElholm said he had met with police and Derry's City Centre Initiative recently to discuss the issue of street begging. Chief Inspector Johnny Hunter, of the Police Service of Northern Ireland, said street begging "is dealt with in a sensitive and proactive manner by police and the appropriate agencies."

"Where those people we find on the street are vulnerable and in need of help, we will work with our partner agencies to keep them safe."

According to the BBC, McElholm said local officers also worked closely with colleagues in the Modern Slavery Human Trafficking Unit. "Where there is evidence of exploitation or of other offenses we will take the necessary appropriate action."

HOT HAND LUKE

In the 1967 movie *Cool Hand Luke*, Paul Newman's character, Luke Jackson, is sentenced to two years in prison for cutting the tops off parking meters. Unfortunately for "Aaron," Hollywood is a far cry from reality: when Aaron, out on parole, was caught stealing the heads off almost eighty parking meters in Texas, he was sentenced to fourteen years behind bars.

According to the *Fort Worth Star-Telegram*, over several weeks in early 2017, police discovered seventy-nine parking meters in various downtown locations missing their heads, and sometimes their poles as well. A special police detail ended the crime spree in March when officers saw Aaron hiding in the shadows and running back and forth across a street. They had been able to track him down because of the loud noises he produced when beating the parking meter heads off with metal water-meter covers. Aaron attempted to flee, but was captured.

Aaron had previously been arrested for burglary of a building, stealing from a coin-operated machine and drug possession, the *Star-Telegram* reported.

A SUCKER BORN EVERY MINUTE

You would be hard-pressed to find someone who cared, or even noticed, the phasing out of the New York City subway token back in the early 2000s. Except for one group of people. They definitely noticed. And considering how they made their living, they undoubtedly cared as well.

On official documents, the crime this group committed was designated as theft of Transit Authority property. Informally, it was known as token-sucking. The criminal would jam the token slot with a piece of paper and lie in wait for a prospective subway rider to insert a token. The token would get stuck, and the annoyed token user would give up and walk away. That's when the token-suck would strike. He would emerge from the shadows of the subway station, place his mouth over the token slot and suck up his reward: a $1.50 token.

As *The New York Times* once put it, "Even among hardened police officers, it was widely considered the most disgusting nonviolent crime that could be committed."

"It gave you the willies," said one veteran transit police officer. "We've had cases every so often, these guys would end up choking and swallowing the tokens. Then what do you do? You've got to wait for the evidence to come out?"

Thankfully, it was rarely ever so dire, as most token-suckers wound up with enough stolen tokens on them to warrant an arrest. The more skilled thieves were able to suck out more than $50 worth of tokens in one day.

Still, it doesn't seem like a hefty reward, considering the germ-covered cost—and the risk of a burning mouth. One subway clerk, according to the *Times*, would sprinkle chili powder in the slots to deter would-be suckers.

CHINESE CHILDREN TAKE A BOW

In June 2017, Chinese authorities attempted to enforce a ban on tiny crossbows, which in the first half of 2017 had become wildly popular with children in China. The so-called toothpick crossbows are designed to shoot small items, like toothpicks, but can also fire nails and needles. The toys work like regular crossbows, but are much smaller. A *Live Science* report noted that they can launch projectiles as far as 30 to 40 feet.

Online videos show that, in addition to their long range, these projectiles are also able to strike with a decent amount of force. Tests conducted by the *Shanghai Daily* found that they could easily pierce cardboard and pop balloons, and one video shows a projectile shattering a light bulb.

And because the toys are small and easy to hide, kids could take the crossbows with them to school.

Concerned parents pointed out that the devices could easily blind someone if used recklessly. "These tiny crossbows can launch sharp projectiles that can cause bodily harm to others, especially injury to the eye," said Dr. Gary Smith, president of the Child Injury Prevention Alliance. "These are not appropriate to be marketed as toys for children."

Soon after this statement, Chinese authorities acted, according to the official Xinhua news agency, which declared that the mini-crossbows had "vanished from shelves almost as fast as they emerged." It quoted one worried Beijing parent as saying, "This is more a time bomb than a toy."

"Business owners shouldn't sell toys that are physically or mentally harmful to minors," said the Administration for Industry and Commerce of Chengdu, in the provincial capital of Sichuan. "Once found, the products will be pulled from the shelves, and the businesses will be punished."

Xinhua quoted an unnamed inspector with the Beijing Municipal Bureau of Commerce, who warned: "Kids are being watched by teachers and parents. Playing with such a toy will not be tolerated. It is too dangerous."

The crossbows have also been pulled from major shopping websites, the agency said, adding that only one injury had been reported in connection with the crossbows in China. A ten-year-old boy in Xinjiang sustained what is likely permanent damage after a projectile launched by a mini-crossbow hit him in the eye.

In China, regular crossbows can be carried around only with a permit, and failure to have a permit can result in five days behind bars and a 500-yuan fine, Xinhua said.

Though China cracked down on the distribution of mini-crossbows, there seem to be no specific laws regarding them in the United States. But none of the listings for them are active on Amazon, which suggests that the online retail giant voluntarily closed the listings.

TAKE THAT, PERVERTS

Another popular but dangerous device in China was the "anti-pervert flamethrower" that could be carried in a handbag. According to *Vice*, a small one would be the size and shape of a cigarette lighter and emit small flames. Larger ones could launch a 20-inch flame with temperatures of up to 3,300 degrees Fahrenheit.

The flamethrowers were on sale for anywhere from $15 to $50 on e-commerce sites.

Chinese police warned that the devices were illegal, as they were weapons, and told Chinese media that it was "technically illegal" to send the devices to customers by mail, *Vice* explained.

But one vendor cited by *The Telegraph* argued that they "can leave a permanent scar, but are a legal, non-lethal tool. Not a weapon."

"Flames and the super high temperatures are enough to scare the bad guys away," said one website, adding that the flames could last up to thirty minutes.

The *Beijing Youth Daily* said the devices became "very popular" when concern over sexual harassment peaked at the start of summer, with some stores selling up to 300 a month.

Authorities were worried that the flamethrowers might injure those carrying them, as the switch could be turned on accidentally when bumped around in a bag, *The Telegraph* reported.

The item's popularity has waned, apparently. Recent online searches could not find any currently available for sale.

FALL FROM GRACE

It all started in June 2018, when an Edmonton, Alberta, couple tried to use a stolen credit card at a Reddi Mart. The convenience store's owner called the police to report the stolen card, and an officer from the Royal Canadian Mounted Police arrived while the two suspects were still in the store.

The Mounties said the man pushed the woman at the first officer on the scene, and the pair of them allegedly fought the officer, trying to resist arrest.

According to the *Mirror*, while the officer caught and subdued the male—who didn't give up easily—the female ran to the back of the store, climbed a ladder and crawled into the ceiling space, hoping to evade capture. But after more police arrived, she fell through the ceiling onto a shelf, and was quickly put under arrest.

The RCMP said the store owner helped the responding officer with arresting both suspects, and nobody involved received any significant injuries.

A twenty-eight-year-old man was charged with eleven offenses, including using a stolen credit card, resisting arrest from the police, resisting arrest from someone aiding the police (the store owner), assaulting a police officer, attempting to disarm a police officer, possession of stolen property under $5,000, mischief under $5,000 and breaching probation.

A twenty-nine-year-old woman was charged with obstructing a police officer, failing to comply and mischief under $5,000.

In July, the woman received a fifteen-day sentence, but got credit for time served and was free to go. The man had not yet been sentenced at the time of writing.

OH, THAT OLD CHESTNUT

Eleven century-old trees—a mature oak, a beech and several sweet chestnuts—were protected by a tree-preservation order made by Poole Borough Council in Dorset, England, in 2001. But scrap-metal magnate "Declan," sixty-seven, didn't care. In February 2018, he took a chainsaw to the trees, thereby increasing the size of his backyard and the amount of sunlight it received—and illegally adding an estimated £137,500 to the value of his £1.4 million, five-bedroom house.

He might have thought he got away with it, but in April 2019, in Southampton Crown Court, Hampshire, a judge confiscated that £137,500 under a Proceeds of Crime Order, and added a £12,000 fine for cutting down the trees, £20,000 in costs and a victim surcharge of £170, bringing Declan's fines to a total of £169,670.

Judge Jane Rowley said Declan had "full knowledge" that the trees were protected, but "deliberately" cut them down to add a "considerable advantage" to the property he had built on a five-acre plot in an affluent area of Dorset.

Furthermore, the court heard that Declan had previously been given a warning by Poole Borough Council after he violated a tree preservation order in 2015.

Declan, the former director of a £2 million scrap-metal business now run by his wife admitted willful destruction of protected trees.

As reported by *Express*, Declan claimed he had cut down the eleven trees, on the east side of his land, because he feared that branches would fall on his grandchildren and because he was "impatient."

But Judge Rowley said there was "overwhelming evidence" that the house's value had been increased by the trees' removal. Surveyors found that significant changes had been made to the house and yard, including the enlargement of the terrace. The removal of the trees, the judge said, allowed Declan "to enjoy a bespoke property."

She added, "You had full knowledge of the tree-preservation order, having previously worked with the council. You were given a clear warning in the past—your actions to cut the trees were criminal."

LOOSE ENDS

I'LL TAKE DOOR NUMBER THREE

Security cameras fantastically captured a break-in at a restaurant in Edinburgh, Scotland, recording the thieves' epic failure.

In January 2018, the *Daily Record* reported that surveillance cameras at the Café Tartine had caught the trio smashing the glass front door and beelining for the back room where the safe was kept, demonstrating that they had done their homework and developed a plan. However, when they got to the door of the back room, their plan began to fall apart. The door wouldn't open. They charged it, kicked it and pounded it, with no result.

By the time they did, eventually, get the door open, the restaurant's alarm system was raising hell, and the three thieves fled with nothing to show for their efforts.

The gang's advance planning seems to have been thorough: they even went so far as to wear matching gray tracksuits. But they made a total mess of the execution. Café Tartine's manager described them as "at the amateur end of the criminal spectrum."

Here's the play-by-play of the whole sorry sequence of events caught on video:

After loitering around outside the glass door of the brasserie, the thieves first tried to pull open the door by its handle. Finally, one of them smashed the glass with a crowbar. They ran inside, where another camera caught them heading straight for the café's rear office.

But they soon discovered that kicking open a door is not as easy as it looks on television. All three tried to knock the office door down, and one of them ran at the door before launching a kick. He failed. Two of them backed up to the door and tried to back-kick it, with no luck. One man tried the crowbar on the door and was joined by a second man with a crowbar. They ended their routine by trying one more time to kick in the door.

When the door suddenly burst open, the trio used flashlights to look around, but quickly realized they couldn't even get into any drawers, let alone a safe. Finally, obviously fretting about the restaurant's security alarm, the bungling burglars made a run for it.

The surveillance footage ends as they file out by way of the smashed front door.

The café's manager said, "They literally got nothing, but it was as if it was all planned, as they knew where the office was and headed straight for it, not taking anything or looking anywhere for anything else.... They didn't get a bean, not a single thing."

CONNECT THE DOTS

A heavy-set man in polka-dot pants was caught on surveillance camera in the middle of an embarrassing attempt to rob a convenience store in Redding, California, in March 2015.

The video, reposted by the *Daily Mail*, shows the man walking by a closed grocery store late at night and stopping to look in through the glass doors. He walked away but returned quickly, this time wearing a black stocking as a mask—though his face had been clearly visible when he looked through the glass previously, and he hadn't bothered to change his distinctive white-on-black polka-dot pants.

Next, he threw a rock at the window. The glass cracked, but didn't break. The store's alarm started, and the man ran off, but not before tripping over a concrete parking curb.

Police, who responded to the store's alarm at about 1 a.m., were quoted by the *Daily Mail* saying that the would-be robber was about 5 foot, 11 inches tall and weighed about 350 pounds. And then there were those pants.

DO NOT PASS GU

In some ways, it was a textbook burglary. In other ways, not so much.

Police in Indio, California, saw security video in September 2016 of a man stealthily entering the YMCA Child Development Center by crawling through the ductwork, dropping to the floor from the ceiling, emptying the drawer of the first cash register he came to, then leaving by the front door, *9News* reported.

But his target was a toy cash register full of play money.

Okay, even if the guy didn't notice that the register was awfully flimsy, you might think he'd notice that the bills, which were not very realistic, were toy money.

Nevertheless, a police spokesman said it was likely that the thief was a professional burglar: "Thieves tend to have specific MOs, with stuff that they follow and stuff that they are comfortable with. They don't get caught doing it once, and they figure, 'Hey, it's a tried-and-true method,' and then they stick to it."

IN JEEP SHIT

It was an ambitious plan, there is no doubt about that. As it turned out, too ambitious.

CNN reported that in October 2012 a group of suspected smugglers tried to use ramps to drive their SUV full of goods over a 14-foot border fence. Unsurprisingly, they had to abandon the scheme, and the car, when the vehicle got stuck on top of the fence.

A border patrol spokesman said agents patrolling the United States–Mexico border near the Imperial Sand Dunes in California's southeast corner spotted the Jeep just after midnight, teetering atop the fence about five miles west of the Colorado River and the Arizona state line. Two men on the Mexican side of the border were trying to free the Jeep, which was empty of cargo, when the agents approached. The men ran farther into Mexico and escaped.

CHAIN OF FOOL

One not-too-bright criminal set out to steal an ATM, but managed only to mess it up over and over again.

The wannabe robber, wearing a mask and gloves, was caught on surveillance cameras in May 2015 when he turned up at a service station near Townsville, Australia, in the middle of the night with a stolen utility truck and a chain, the Australian Broadcasting Corporation reported. After attaching the chain to the ATM, the untalented thief started to drive away. But he soon realized he had never attached the other end of the chain to the truck! He stopped the truck and tried to connect the chain to it, but he was now too far away from the cash machine, and the chain wasn't long enough to reach the truck.

After that, Queensland Police said, he gave up and drove across the road to another service station, where he threw a slab of concrete at the door in an attempt to break it. When that didn't work, he smashed the glass with a hammer and made his way inside. It's unknown if this second attempt yielded any loot.

NOTHING LIKE A GOOD PUB CRAWL

A man in Queensland, Australia, might take the cake for the most poorly executed break-in.

In surveillance footage released by the targeted bar, the thief can be seen repeatedly hitting the glass door with a beer keg. After several strikes, he created a hole just big enough for his body to slide through. And by "just big enough," we mean *just big enough*. The hole was awkwardly located a third of the way up the door, but the man wiggled his way through and then fell, ungracefully, onto the floor inside the bar. As he got up, he kicked the door, which caused it to swing open—he had broken the door frame and could have just walked right in.

As *NBC Bay Area* reported, after all that effort the man apparently realized he was not going to be able to steal any beer, so he left.

In a Facebook post, the owners said: "We were broken into at 3:30 a.m. this morning, if that's what you would call it." They jokingly asked if anyone was able to recognize "this idiot."

HOLD THIS, WILL YA?

A gun-wielding thief raided a London bank in October 2011, demanding £700,000 in cash from the man behind the counter. But then, in a colossal gaffe, the robber, disguised only with sunglasses and a cap, handed his gun to the teller instead of a bag, reported *The Telegraph*.

The teller and the crook both froze as the robber realized his mistake. Then the crook grabbed the gun back and ran away as the bank's security shutters came down and bank staff hit the alarm button.

The thief escaped by stealing a bank worker's bike and pedaling off.

The bank eventually put up a £25,000 reward for information about the robbery, and police released a security video of the man just before he entered the bank.

A police spokesman said, "This man is not the sharpest tool in the box. The guess is that he is very inexperienced and panicked when he approached the cashier, handing over his gun instead of a bag by mistake."

KEYSTONE CROOK

In his excitement at robbing a 7-Eleven convenience store, a San Diego man made the mistake all car owners fear: he locked his keys inside the car. Besides being a generally annoying and time-consuming error to fix, it nearly ruined his escape plan. Upon realizing his gaffe as he left the store, *NBC 26 Green Bay* reported, the robber panicked and smashed the car window. He then proceeded to climb into the car through the window, a task one can only imagine must have been difficult and uncomfortable.

Despite seeming to have everything working against him, the man successfully escaped, and there has been no recent update on his whereabouts.

Maybe this guy wasn't as dumb as we thought. Maybe.